OUTSIDE
THE GATE

Illustration facing: detail from 'The Gates of the City of London',
tapestry designed by John Piper, hanging in the entrance of
Sedgewick Group PLC, Aldgate.

First published June 1994
by STEPNEY BOOKS
19 Tomlins Grove, London E3 4NX
Copyright © Malcolm Johnson 1994
Illustrations © David Hoffmann, Tim Mills, David Shenton
Cover: Sally Fentiman

British Library Cataloguing in Publication Data. A catalogue record
for this book is available from the British Library.

ISBN 0 9523404 02

Set in Caslon 3 and 540
Printed by Expression Printers Ltd, London N5 1JT

IF YOU HAVE
A WORTHWHILE
CAUSE WE'LL TAKE
IT UNDER OUR WING

EAGLE STAR
COVERS YOUR WORLD

INVESTMENT · INSURANCE · PENSIONS

National Westminster Bank
We're here to make life easier

NATIONAL WESTMINSTER BANK . AT THE HEART OF THE COMMUNITY .

National Westminster Bank is pleased to be associated with St. Botolph's and its excellent work with London's homeless.

RICHARDS BUTLER
and ST BOTOLPH'S

City lawyers Richards Butler have been associated with St Botolph's Church since moving to its offices in Beaufort House some four years ago. For nearly 75 years the practice of Richards Butler has had close associations with life in the City and has been delighted to support the St. Botolph's Project. During the last few years the firm's 550 staff have held an annual Carol Service in the Church.

Richards Butler participates in the Aldgate Business Houses Council and has organised a number of fund raising events for various appeals. A performance by the Covent Garden Minuet Company was held in the offices of Richards Butler to raise funds for St. Botolph's.

RICHARDS BUTLER
Beaufort House
15 St Botolph Street
London EC3A 7EE
Tel: 071-247 6555
Tlx: 949494 RBLAW G
Fax: 071-247 5091

LONDON • PARIS • BRUSSELS • ABU DHABI • HONG KONG

OUTSIDE THE GATE

St Botolph's and Aldgate
950 – 1994

Malcolm Johnson

 Stepney Books

For Robert

Contents

Acknowledgements

I am grateful to Mr Peter Scott and to these members of the Aldgate Business Houses Council:

Barclays Bank PLC
Barlow Lyde and Gilbert
Eagle Star Insurance Group
Guardian Royal Exchange Assurance PLC
CE Heath PLC
IT Planning and Finance
National Westminster Bank PLC
Richards Butler
The Sedgwick Group PLC

who have generously underwritten the cost of this book so that all money from sales can go to the work of St Botolph's Centre.

I also owe a huge debt to my secretary Matt Sexton who has patiently typed and re-typed the manuscript for this book. He is now an authority on Aldgate. Jenny Smith has been a supportive editor, David Hoffmann and Tim Mills have taken several of the excellent photographs. Most of *Local Villains* is taken from Donald Rumbelow's books, *The Houndsditch Murders* and *Jack the Ripper* and I thank him for allowing me to use these. My friend David Shenton, one of the cartoonists of *The Guardian* generously gave me *The Tight Rope Walker* and the drawing of Aldgate. I also thank Ivy Walker, Brother Jude Hill, and Graham Brandreth Wills.

Finally I thank the Revd Victor Stock and the Revd Brian Lee for their excellent contributions. Relations between successor and predecessor can often be difficult but Brian has shown me extraordinary kindness and I am so glad he is at Aldgate.

MALCOLM JOHNSON
April 1994

LIST OF ILLUSTRATIONS

Frontispiece: The Gates of the City of London

❖ FOREWORD

At the end of Malcolm Johnson's incumbency as Rector of St
Botolph's Aldgate a deeply moving service of farewell was held,
referred to in this book but without the following anecdote. I was one of
the enormous congregation which packed the nave, aisles, galleries with
extra chairs and people standing just inside the door. It was a most
beautifully and imaginatively worked out service. Bankers and lawyers in
City pinstripes, the homeless looking down from the gallery and the
workers looking up from the crypt, the gay community, the local schools,
the Jewish community were a panorama of humanity only to be found in
God's Kingdom. There were very few dry eyes as the Rector made his way
out of the church and in the silence that descended a lone voice was heard
'Anyone got a f...... tissue?' Somehow that struck absolutely the right note.

This book is about the notes which make up the Aldgate song, some
horribly jarring from the gruesome Jack the Ripper to the appalling siege
of Sidney Street, violence, poverty, homelessness, destitution, all these
notes struck again and again. But from the beginning this place outside
the gate at the crossroads has been a place of holiness. Perhaps that is one
of the evidences of authentic Christian faith and life - where there is pain,
sorrow and need there is God.

The story of Aldgate is the story of people from the Poor Clare's nuns
in the convent at the Minories founded in 1293 by Queen Blanche to the
Franciscans serving in the parish today, as part of Malcolm Johnson's
extraordinarily talented team. Bishops, like Gerald Ellison, the last great
prelatical patrician gaitered episcopal figure in a Church of England now
past, who despite everything became such an imaginative and strategically
important figure, supportive of 'the pastoral initiatives' undertaken in the
face of prudence and career prospects by the last incumbent. Indeed it
was in the glittering ambiance of the Mansion House that Fr Percy
Coleman, once like Malcolm Johnson Area Dean of the City, took me
aside into a window embrasure and said 'there'll be no preferment for
Malcolm, I'm afraid he has pursued certain pastoral initiatives.'

These pastoral initiatives of course were Malcolm Johnson's work with
the Lesbian and Gay Community in London and beyond and the story of
the Diocese of London and its dealings with the LGCM. Archdeacon,
Chancellor and Bishop evicting that community from the St Botolph's
church tower is a stain on the honour and integrity of the Diocese of

London which will long remain. The chapter telling that story is a particularly upsetting one.

But what a place! How can the reader not warm to a parish that produces a beadle called Mr Smallcoal and an incumbent call Dr Fly, rector incidentally for 63 years until 1873 whilst also being Vicar of Willesden. In 1551 the Lord Mayor discovered there were 40 aliens resident in Aldgate many of them heretics 'as well as women and children,' for women and children hardly mattered. St Botolph's Aldgate shines like a star in the Christian firmament because it has always been a place for the alien, marginalised, oppressed, the unnoticed, the discarded. St Botolph's has served all throughout its history the needs of those women and men most dear to Jesus Christ who himself 'died without the gate'. Aldgate is a crossroads and a gateway and it surprised me reading the book to discover that John Piper when asked to make a stained glass window about heaven he didn't know how to go about it. All the great artist needed to do was look around him, for Christopher Wren's epitaph in the Crypt of St Paul's surely stands as the motto and clarion call of St Botolph, Aldgate today with those famous words applied to Christ himself for those who seek evidence of his existence and his power. 'If you seek his monument look around you.' This monument is the people of Aldgate, the children in the school, the homeless in the crypt, the gay couple being affirmed and loved, the Jewish refugee, the Muslim neighbour, the City financier, the grandee and the pauper. If this history of Aldgate fails to open a window into heaven the reader will be unimaginative indeed for 'here is none other than the House of God, this is the Gate of Heaven.'

VICTOR STOCK
Rector
St Mary-le-Bow
15th February 1994

PART ONE

History

1 INTRODUCTION

Past and Present

On the morning of 29 August 1990 the workmen renovating the south vault of St Botolph's called me to the room below the Baptistry where they were lowering the floor to give more headroom. They had dug up the remains of Mrs Mary Hague, who had died on 24 August, 1812, aged 56. The coffin wood had disintegrated, the skull, still with wig like hair on it, was separated from the bones of the body. I asked them to reverently rebury it and said a prayer. A few hours later the huge Irish navvy, all smiles, came to my study and reported that he had found a male skeleton. 'I have put them together so they should be happy now.'

In Aldgate the past rarely impinges on the present but during the nearly nineteen years I was rector of St Botolph's I was continually reminded of the many men and women who had lived, worked or just passed through the parish since the first Saxon church was built at the old gate around 950 AD. Today Aldgate is a place of contrasts and contradictions because to the east of the church lies Tower Hamlets, a Borough with all the challenges of the inner city, containing people from many different ethnic, religious and cultural backgrounds and to the west lies the City with its immense wealth and business acumen. Only five thousand people live in the Square Mile but over three hundred thousand people pour in each day to work in the banks and business houses. They hurry from the tube to the office rarely sparing a thought for their predecessors who lived a very different sort of life. I hope this book might bring the past and present together.

At the centre of Aldgate, marooned on an island where eight roads meet, is the parish church presiding over the traffic noise and chaos. St Botolph's values the past but does not live in it so today there is definite work to be done and definite needs to fill. Known as the Travellers' Church because people pass by on their journeys in and out of the City, its daily worship attempts to remind us of another journey – the journey to God. Its steeple points to 'The Other', not despising the world of money, markets and marriages but giving them meaning and direction. Its historic organ and bells play for the General Dance, bidding us join in.

I came to Aldgate as Rector in 1974 little realising what I was in for. I thought I was inheriting a quiet City church from which I could do my counselling work. I had been a curate in the busy parish of St Mark, Portsea, Portsmouth then a University chaplain at Queen Mary College, part of London University, in the Mile End Road. At my Induction Service the Bishop of London, Gerald Ellison reprimanded me for delaying the start of the service and keeping him waiting. I explained that I had opened the lavatory door and a very drunk homeless man had fallen out hitting his head so I had administered emergency first aid. The Bishop was not impressed nor was I when I later saw our verger chasing the man out of the churchyard, threatening him with the large silver mace. So much for hospitality. Surely we could do better than that.

The 'quiet little parish' turned out for me to be place of many demands and needs. Its tiny geographical area has only a small resident population, most of whom are Muslim or Jewish and in 1974 a tiny Sunday congregation most of whom were odd – like me. I thought that seemed promising and we would probably get on well together. In this book I have described what happened and put it in the context of the parish's one thousand years history. I discovered all of human life is here and at rush hour would often stand on the church steps gazing out at the hundreds of business people hurrying home with their briefcases, university students making their way to a lecture, homeless men and women stumbling down our crypt steps in ever increasing numbers, the local residents going shopping in Petticoat Lane and school children running home with their satchels. Tourists looking for the Tower of London had no idea they were standing on the site of Chaucer's house or the place where Queen Mary and her sister Queen Elizabeth I had passed by in a grand procession to the ringing of St Botolph's bells.

Controversy is a daily guest at St Botolph's as the parish immerses itself in some of the big issues confronting today's Church. The ordination of women to the priesthood, the obscenity of homelessness, the challenge of the HIV virus and the fight against homophobia are but some of the areas of concern. It means much media attention most of which is unwelcome but I did like the description of 'St Botolph's without Windows' in the satirical *Not the Church Times* which announced that our regular Sunday Worship is a Charismatic Bondage Service at 3 pm. Our opponents are vocal but so are our supporters and, thank God, the congregation is surrounded by hundreds of helpers and volunteers without whom nothing could be done.

I have not been able to discover the consecration date of the present church building but the 250th anniversary falls in 1994. This book is a modest gift to the parish, a thank offering for a happy incumbency.

2 THE PARISH

A Thousand Years of History

The parish church of Aldgate is probably of Saxon foundation. One historian thinks it was built by Sired, Dean of St Paul's before the Norman Conquest but the origins are lost in the mists of time. We do know that from very early times a church stood outside the old or ald gate in the Roman wall surrounding the City.

It is remarkable so little is known about St Botolph as around sixty churches mainly in East Anglia are named after him, and Boston is 'Botolph's Town.' The earliest reference to Botolph is a notice in the *Anglo-Saxon Chronicle*, 'In 654 King Anna was killed and Botwulf began to build a monastery at Icanhoh.' In 670 Abbot Ceolfrith of Wearmouth visited Botolph and so established a link with the north of England. The Venerable Bede does not mention him but Folchard, the Abbot of Thorny near Peterborough at the time of the Norman Conquest, compiled a *Life of Botolph* which obviously must be part legend as it was written 400 years after the Saint's death. Folchard records that two brothers Adulph and Botolph became monks and went to France where Adulph became a Bishop. Botolph returned to England and encouraged by Ethelmund, King of the South Angles founded a Benedictine monastery at Ikanhoe said to be near Aldeburgh in Suffolk. A less likely theory is that Botolph is buried at Hadstock near Saffron Walden in Essex. The main reason for connecting Icanhoh with Hadstock is a reference in the *Book of Ely* which describes Cadenho, the medieval name for Hadstock, as 'that place which was consecrated to religion long ago by the Holy Botolph, there at rest' but the connection cannot be proved despite traces of late Saxon work.

The monastery was destroyed by the Danes in 963 when the relics of the saint were removed some to Ely and some to Thorney. Other relics were given to Edward the Confessor for his Abbey at Westminster.

Botolph was a humble mild man, apparently well known for his hospitality, so after his death in 655 he became the Patron Saint of Travellers. His day in the calendar is 17 June, and the collect is:

'O God, the guide and governor of all kingdoms, who dost grant to thy servants yearly to celebrate the festival of Botolph thy Confessor and Abbot; take from us we pray the scars of our wounds and heal us with the gifts of our heavenly fatherland.'

The eastern edge of the City had always been vulnerable to attack particularly by the Danes arriving in their boats on the Thames. In 967 thirteen Knights in the retinue of King Edgar asked the King to grant them a parcel of land where they might live and at the same time defend the eastern edge of the city. The historian Stow says the King demanded that each knight perform some brave deed above ground under ground and under water. This was done and they were summoned to the tilt yard in East Smithfield (near the present World Trade Centre) to take on all comers. No one came and the King dubbed them the Knighten Guild and the boundaries of their Land were fixed. It is the land of the present parish of St Botolph together with East Smithfield, the present St Katharine's Dock and as far into the Thames 'as a horseman could enter at low water and throw his spear.' Successive Kings, – Ethelred, Canute, Edward the Confessor and William the Conqueror, confirmed the privileges. William Rufus's charter is extant and was confirmed by Henry I. This is the area now known as Portsoken Ward. In 1107 Norman, the Prior of Aldgate, founded a monastery just inside Aldgate and for some reason in 1125 the descendents of the thirteen knights surrendered their soke to the Prior of the new Monastery of Holy Trinity on condition they were made canons. We know the names of the men who suddenly made this momentous change and we know who the witnesses to the ceremony were. One of them was Orgare le Prude who was deputed to go and tell the King what had happened. The Prior was put in charge of St Botolph's church, the principal building of the Soke. The Prior also now became the Alderman of the Ward. The Prior/Rector/Alderman obviously enjoyed his temporal and spiritual power and was seen riding with 'the mayor and his brethren. The Alderman as one of them in scarlet or other livery as they used.' Stow says the cut of his garment was slightly different to denote his ecclesiastical status. We know the Prior was present at the second election of R Whittington as Lord Mayor, on 13 October 1406. From the Norman Conquest onwards the Rector was a force to be reckoned with in the City Corporation. My membership of the City's Education Committee looked very feeble in comparison.

In 1157 Withulph, a priest of Aldgate, had a dispute with the priest of St Peter of the Bailey. It was an unseemly quarrel over who should bury Godluna, wife of Eilric. The Archdeacon declared in favour of St Botolph and Ralph the Prior received a pall, and one chensa and six sheep as the fee.

By the reign of Edward III the City had fixed its boundaries which extended beyond the City walls and gates to the bars. In Aldgate the bar was 100 yards east of the gate and is commemorated today by a marble plinth with a dragon holding the City coat of arms. Travellers paid the dues on their goods at the Bar, this was then raised and they proceeded through the gate into the City itself. St Botolph's was between the gate and the bar hence its title 'St Botolph without Aldgate.' The other three medieval churches who adopted Botolph as their patron were also outside their gates – Aldersgate, Bishopsgate, (both still functioning as churches), and Billingsgate which was destroyed in the Great Fire.

Medieval Aldgate was a noisy bustling busy place. The gate was the focus of attention because there tolls were collected for the upkeep of City roads. In the 13th century tolls were levied to repair roads although the amount charged seems to vary. A hired cart with wool or hides or other merchandise had to pay twopence, but twopence halfpenny if it entered 'by Holbourne or by the Flete or by Allgate'. In 1356 a smaller amount was levied because carts caused 'great damage and are in peril of losing what they bring because that the roads without the gates are so torn up and the pavements so broken.' If you were bringing food for your own use you paid nothing.

We know that the gate was in a ruinous condition in 1215 because Robert Fitz Walter, the leader of the Barons opposed to King John, marched with his army from Ware arriving on 24 May passing through the gate with no opposition at all because many people were apparently in church. The gate was pulled down and rebuilt in the Norman style soon afterwards. It was of double construction, the outer part having tall towers on which were exhibited the heads of those who had been executed nearby. In 1282 two sergeants were ordered to be on duty at each of the city gates and this was complied with at Aldgate.

Until 1386 private tenants were given a lease to hire rooms above the City gates and in 1374 a lease was granted to Geoffrey Chaucer who at the time was comptroller of the Customs and Subsidy of Wool, Skins and Tanned Hides in the Port of London. His was a life tenancy on a full repairing lease reserving the right of re-entry 'in time of defence of the City aforesaid so often as it shall be necessary.'

Seven years later such a situation occurred during the Peasants' Revolt. The Aldgate, said the Lord Mayor, was to be guarded day and night 'by four men sufficiently well armed, and four archers of the people of your Ward; that so no stranger enter there through the same, with any armor, unless he be a gentleman or else an archer who will say upon his faith that he has now come unto our said Lord the King .'

About 1400 an ugly scene took place outside the church when a man from Brittany murdered a widow of Aldgate who had taken pity on him and allowed him to lodge with her. He had been ordered by the magistrate to return to his country but the local women had other ideas and stopped him as he left the City and stoned him to death.

Little is known about the earliest St Botolph's church but in 1418 due to the increase in population it was considerably enlarged. An aisle was added called 'the new Ile of St Katharine', and a new tower and another chapel were built. The donor was Robert Burford a wealthy bell founder. By the early sixteenth century the church had to be completely rebuilt 'at the special charges of the Priory of Holy Trinity.' The number of parishioners had greatly increased again, 'the church is pestered with lofts and seats for them.' A larger building was needed.

Much excitement occured in 1471 when 5,000 men led by the Bastard Falconbridge during the Wars of the Roses, stormed the Gate on King Edward's behalf. A few men got into the City but the portcullis was lowered and they were slain. The Alderman of Aldgate Ward with a body of troops then sallied forth from the gate and pushed the invaders back to St Botolph's. Further troops from the Tower routed the men chasing them to Mile End, Poplar and Stratford.

A useful manuscript for scholars of medieval Aldgate is now in the Guildhall Library (No 260). Completed by William Black in 1833 it lists the 82 deeds and other papers relating to wills and documents of tenements bequeathed to provide chantry chapels in the 14th and 15th centuries. The deeds are kept in the Cottonian Library. Masses were arranged to be said by a 'fit' priest (meaning not healthy but fitting) in the chapels for the deceased benefactor.

The Reformation in the 16th century and particularly the dissolution of religious houses had a profound effect throughout England. There was great upheaval in Aldgate as Holy Trinity Priory was dissolved in 1531 and the Convent of the Poor Clares closed eight years later. At a stroke Henry VIII destroyed most of the provision the monasteries had made for the poor. Now the vestries of parishes were to be the unit of local government with all the responsibilities that that meant.

When King Henry VIII died and his young Protestant son Edward VI came to the throne it was rumoured that all the trappings of Catholic worship would be confiscated leaving each parish with only one vessel for the Communion Service. Churchwardens in the City began to sell their plate including the wily wardens of Aldgate. In 1552 the Royal Commissioners asked all the City churches to account for the handling of their property since the beginning of the reign. The wardens admitted selling two chalices, a pair of cruets, a pair of altar candlesticks, an altar cross, a pair of censers, an incense boat with spoon, one pyx, two basins and two paxs. Such a wealth of plate would have been incredible in an English provincial church but was not exceptional in the City. With the money realised the wardens had bought a paten and a non ecclesiastical standing cup and cover weighing 32½ oz. Vestments and church furniture from Holy Trinity came to St Botolph's and in 1551 an auction was held of Latin service books, rich copes and priceless plate. Much merriment accompanied the sale and in the churchwarden's account book there is an entry 'Paid for beer and ale, the 21st day of May when the parish was selling the ornaments and vestments . . . 6d.'

When King Edward was succeeded by his Catholic sister, Mary in 1553 Aldgate was well placed to re-equip the church for the Old Services. The earliest piece of plate possessed today bears a 1559 hallmark. On her accession in 1553 Queen Mary entered London through Aldgate accompanied by a body of 2,000 on horseback. The Queen and Princess Elizabeth, her sister, entered St Botolph's for prayer. Fourpence was paid to peal the bells and gravel was spread before the church door.

A year later Mary committed her sister Elizabeth to the Tower but after two months allowed her to move to Woodstock. By chance when the order of release arrived at the Tower the Princess was standing by an open window listening the the 'merry bells' of Aldgate. Soon afterwards she presented the church with a set of silken bell ropes in remembrance of the occasion of her release. Fragments of the ropes were around in 1834 but none remain today. When Elizabeth came to the throne in 1558 there was another reversal of church policy and the protestant service was once again brought into use.

One of Aldgate's most famous residents Edmund Spenser, the poet, was born locally in 1552. From now onwards we are well supplied with information as the parish records, which are very extensive indeed and now lodged in the Guildhall Library, include churchwarden accounts from 1547, registers of baptisms, marriages and burials from 1558 and record books of day to day happenings in the parish from 1583. Thomas Forbes' *Chronicle from Aldgate* (Yale 1971) discusses and lists these in great detail.

Tudor Aldgate was similar to medieval Aldgate – streets and houses crowded with people. It was a poor but very lively community. At the centre of it all was the parish clerk who meticulously noted down the names, ages, address and occupation of parishoners brought for baptism, burial or marriage. Sermons were described, visitations by the bishop noted together with the cost of the banquet afterwards. On one occasion 38 guests sat down to a sumptuous dinner of beef washed down by claret and beer. Occasionally indignation thrust aside discretion as he castigated unwed parents or lazy rogues in his marginal notes. In England weekly lists or bills of mortality were not kept until 1603 and the first census took place in 1801 so the Aldgate records are of immense importance. Forbes has listed the occupations of the 180 fathers of babies who were baptised during 1600. Sailors, coopers and tailors are the most numerous then silk weavers, butchers, draymen and carmen. These all account for 71 of the fathers. The professions requiring some degree of education – lawyer, curate, clerk, doctor, pettifogger (a petty legal practitioner) only account for six fathers.

St Botolph's was an urban parish but fields lay close by so in the records mention is made of shepherds, hogmen, fowlers, gardeners etc. Most numerous were the unskilled inhabitants such as labourers, loaders, porters, maidservants, servingmen and night men (they removed the night soil). In the Records for 18 July 1593 appears Lodovic Bassano one of the Queen's 'musitions'. Perhaps he knew Roger Rafton 'a mad brayned fellow of Houndsditch, free (Member of the Guild of) musitions.' The clerk who listed less admirable persons also included 'Joane Beldam a lewd person' (30 July 1618) and 'Robert Dabbs a Newgatebird' (22 September 1618). In 1586 the clerk recorded the bells rang for joy on 9 February as 'the queene of Skotts was beheaded.' Royal edicts were listed such as that of 17 August 1595 when all householders were urged to possess bows and arrows for everyone under their roof and there is a curious edict listed from the Mayor (1 June 1595) saying the Queen has forbidden the use of blue starch. No one knows why, particularly as white starch was permitted but Forbes suggests it was an anti-plague health measure. Few took notice of Her Majesty's wishes so another similar edict had to be read in church on 27 June 1596.

Robert Heaze or Hayes was parish priest at St Botolph's 1564-94. Many of the record books were kept by him and his writing is clear and beautiful. The spelling, however, has little method. In July, 1580 he writes about hearing the confession of two men, Walter Wrey and Charles Waken 'who were executed at Wapping for robing of a Spanish shipp in the straights.' In 1588 he records that he has so far baptised 3,124 people, buried 4,379 and taken 1,538 weddings! All in 24 years. His wife and grandchild preceeded him to the grave and his last years were full of sorrow. The last entry in his handwriting says

> Heare I conclude and make an ende
> he that lacks money lacks his ffrende

He died 6 April 1594 'of the gravell and the stone' and was buried under the altar.

Communion at that time was administered monthly, but at Easter five communion services were held for between 500 and 700 communicants. In 1583 two gallons of malmsey were consumed but this was greatly exceeded in 1618 when Easter Communions began on Mid Lent Sunday and continued every Sunday till Easter Day and Low Sunday. Claret wine was used this time and between 22 and 28 gallons were consumed. Unfortunately the number of communicants is not mentioned. This huge quantity explains why St Botolph's possessed such capacious silver flagons. Attendance at Easter communion was, of course, compulsory so this should help us know the population of the parish but figures for 1595-99 seem low. Annual baptisms varied between 176 and 221 and burials between 175 and 358; Obviously many people did not enter their parish church at Easter and several may have been temporary residents. Much later figures were given which might help us. Graunt in1759 said that the Ward of Portsoken had a population of 5,703 in 1631 but to this must be added the Liberty of East Smithfield. Rowse (1951) reckons that the whole of London's population in 1600 must have been around 300,000.

The Aldgate clerk always listed the cause of death which had to be ascertained by 'searchers.' These were 'antient matrons, sworn to their office' who at the sound of the bell tolling would hurry to view the corpse. They would then tell the clerk the cause of death. However, not everyone had confidence in these ladies. John Graunt a century later wrote that the old women searchers after the mist of a cup of ale and the bribe of a fourpence fee (instead of the normal two-pence) 'cannot tell whether this emaciation or leanness were from a phthisis (wasting disease) or from an hectic fever, atrophy etc.' Presumably families wished to conceal the presence of plague so were willing to bribe the searchers. Of the deaths recorded between 1583 and 1599 23% were from plague, 22% from consumption and surprisingly only one and one half percent were from childbirth. The prize for longevity, if the record is to be believed goes to Agnis Sadler aged 126 who was buried on 26 April, 1575. She obviously survived every disease the sixteenth century had to offer as did 43 other hardy souls who died of old age, less than 1% of the total. Surgery of the day being what it was it is surprising that so few post-operative deaths are recorded but perhaps the people of Aldgate were too poor to be attended by surgeons. Removing stones (gravel) from the bladder was a hazardous business and Sir William Winter died on 20 February, 1588 'being cutt of the collick and the stone.' Serious depression or anxiety was described as 'taken in a thowgat' and explains the death of eleven men and ten women. The best known was the parish priest himself, Christopher Threlkeld (incumbent 1594-97). Few suicides are mentioned but on 7 September 1590, Amy Stokes who had hung herself, was buried at nine in the evening in a far corner of the churchyard.

In 1606 the old gate was rebuilt under the supervision of Mr Martin Bard. King James I had made his state entry to the City five years earlier and was so pleased by his reception that he gave £500 for gifts to the poor and for the rebuilding of Aldgate; an unusually generous gift for the Scottish King. Accordingly when the gate was at last finished in 1617 an effigy of James was put on it. Ben Jonson in his *Silent Women* complains that those gilding the statues at Aldgate would only work under canvas, presumably because of inclement weather. 'Gilders will not worke but enclosed. How long did the canvas hang before Aldgate?' The gate, when completed must have looked very grand. To the east two statues of soldiers stood as sentinels with a golden sphere and weather vane atop and in the centre the statue of the king in gilt armour. Facing towards the City were the three statues of Peace, Fortune and Charity. These statues had all disappeared by 1761. Aldgate was the place where punishments by City magistrates ended, often in the stocks. Rogues and rascals and common courtesans had to endure taunts and floggings as they passed through the city streets to the eastern boundary. In 1714 a Tory schoolmaster was flogged from the Stocks Market to Aldgate and died of it. It seems a disproportionate punishment even for a schoolmaster. All the City gates were removed under the provision of an Act of Parliament in 1760, the last to disappear being Newgate in 1777. The materials were sold by the City to the highest bidder. Aldgate was sold for £177. 10s. 0d. and the ornaments were taken by Sir Walter Blackett to decorate Rothley Castle in Northumberland. Mr Mussell of Bethnal Green rebuilt part of Aldgate on the north side of his house, Wentworth House, which he renamed, Aldgate House.

A great benefactor of the parish, Mr Robert Dow, was buried in May, 1612. His memorial still stands near the main entrance to the present church having been brought down from the gallery in 1966. The clerk drew a skull at the side of the entry in the parish register 'he is buried in the chancel, he was about 90 years old'. In 1606 Mr Dow gave the church a very handsome chalice made in 1594 and it is still in the church's possession today. His memorial shows him in contemporary cap and ruff leaning on a skull. A generous man he had also provided for 64 poor folk of the parish.

In October of the same year Sir Arthur Darcy, knight of Dartford in Kent was buried in the chancel and his family's memorial (1560) is still to be seen close to that of Mr Dow. It represents a sarcophagus with a recumbent figure upon it. It is a very fine monument indeed, and was set up to commemorate Thomas Darcy who opposed the dissolution of the monasteries and who was executed for treason in 1538 at the Tower.

In 1615 the churchyard was so crowded it was necessary to purchase some land in Rosemary Lane, East Smithfield. The Bishop of London,

John King, came in great style and the service was held in a tent on the new cemetery. The inevitable banquet followed – this time at the house of Sir Allen Apsleies.

The church was repaired and improved between 1620 and 1630 and tradespeople such as fruiterers, herb women and others were told to remove their forms, baskets and boards from the porch and yard. Unlike the present building the old church was built east-west with three aisles of almost equal height and width. To the south was a tower topped by pinnacles and a lantern shape. This was copied when a churchwarden's mace was made and is also seen on the head of the silver mace of the Sir John Cass's Foundation.

The clerk continued to put his own comments beside his entries in the registers. In 1623 he described a couple of 17 and 14 who were married as 'a worthie ancient couple of young fools', of another couple the bride was 'a piece of cracked stuff'. A forward widow, we are told, married 'with much adoe'.

From 1629-35 Aldgate had a fiery, troublesome incumbent. Thomas Edwards had non-conformist tendencies which got him into hot water so he was 'suppressed and suspended' by Archbishop Laud probably for boasting 'I never had a canonical coat, never gave a penny to the building of St Pauls, took not the canonical oath . . . and did not bow at the altar and at the name of Jesus.' His day came when Parliament took over the country but he refused all Livings probably because he had married a wealthy wife and valued his independence. The unrestrained virulence of his language, the intemperate fury with which he attacked all those whose theological opinions varied from his own and his personal attacks on the character of his fellow clergy did not endear him to any but sermon tasters. When he died in 1647 Jeremiah Burroughes wrote 'That fiery rogue, that implacable, irrational violence of his against godly persons makes me stand and wonder.'

The various outbreaks of plague in 1563 and 1593 caused much havoc at St Botolph's. Further epidemics followed in 1603 and 1625. In the latter year one in six of the population died and in the parish of the 2,573 burials 1,653 were plague victims. In 1665 the Great Plague struck killing an estimated 68,596 people in London (see below). Life in these days was certainly short. Forbes reckons that of 100 children born in the 1580s only 48 would survive until their fifth birthday and 27 to the age of ten.

The Commonwealth period was a troubled time for St Botolph's. Its incumbent Thomas Swadlin, instituted in 1635 was a High Churchman and supporter of Archbishop Laud who had come in January, 1631 to consecrate St Katharine Cree Church. Swadlin offended the Puritans after

1   View of St Botolph's, 1722

King Charles had been beheaded so he was deprived of the Living and imprisoned in Newgate. A succession of obscure ministers held the Living until in 1654 Mr John Macarness was chosen by popular election. He was a priest of the Church of England and this angered the Presbyterians and Independents. By the intervention of Cromwell himself he was deposed and a Presbyterian, Zachariah Crofton, was appointed. He was under no illusions about his task. Later he wrote, 'I must not think to rake in a wasps' nest and not be stung.' The Lecturer at this time – also appointed by parishoners – was an Anabaptist who detested 'baby sprinkling.' He was John Simpson and he had hoped to be incumbent himself. Mr Crofton wrote to Simpson telling him not to preach in St Botolph's any more but on Sunday 2 August 1657 an unseemly scene took place. After morning service Crofton remained in the pulpit and continued to preach. He was determined to hold it against all comers. Simpson arrived with several supporters, climbed into the gallery opposite and also started to preach. Two sermons for the price of one. We are not told how the day ended. Fortunately I did not have such fractious lecturers. George Stevens was the gentle, knowledgeable secretary of the London Diocesan Council for Jewish Christian Understanding. On his death John Hunter a retired Australian priest living in Charterhouse won the hearts of everyone by his humour and forthrightness. He died in 1984 and was succeeded by the much loved scholarly Percy Coleman, formerly Rector of St Andrew by the Wardrobe and Area Dean of the City.

A pamphlet war began and things got dirty when Crofton was accused of beating his servant maid. In 1660 the Monarchy was restored, Simpson disappears for ever and Crofton preached a sermon on the 'Pursuit of Peace'. However, as a Presbyterian he continued to criticise episcopacy and at one time there were 2,000 people outside the Tantling Meeting House waiting to hear him 'bang the bishops'. He was imprisoned in the Tower and Thomas Swadlin who had been ejected in 1642 was restored to the incumbency in 1661. Sadly he died within the year so Mr Macarness was summoned to return. Crofton lived on till 1672 and founded a school in Aldgate.

The period under Cromwell was a turbulent time for St Botolph's. Services were still held but often marriages were conducted by the Alderman not the Rector, and different factions in the Church warred against each other.

In 1665 the Great Plague hit London. A vivid account is given by Daniel Defoe in his *Journal of the Plague Year*. He was born only four years before its outbreak but obviously knew and talked with many eye witnesses. Defoe was married in St Botolph's in 1683. He records that two great pits twenty feet deep were dug in the churchyard at the time of the pestilence and we know that the summer months of 1665 brought much suffering. In July there were 217 burials, 1,004 in August, 1,981 in September, 1,742 in October and 192 in November. The incumbent Thomas Arden, later Dean of Chester, unlike other City clergy and doctors stayed at his post. The clerk records that many died 'unknelled, uncoffined and unknown.' The Great Fire which broke out the following year purified the City. Six shillings was paid to carry away the parish books but the fire did not reach Aldgate. We are told a parishoner dropped dead on Tower Hill: 'being affrighted'.

In 1676 Mr Thomas Whiting later Master of the Joiners Company gave to the church the organ built by Renatus Harris which was in his house in Houndsditch and is still in the church.

White Kennett, the only Rector to have a local street named after him, was incumbent from 1700-1707 when the population of the parish was around 24,000. This does not include the parish of Holy Trinity Minories. A very disgruntled man he had an influence on the affairs of the nation as well as the local scene. He opposed the authority of Convocation and wrote several books. He became Dean, then Bishop, of Peterborough. Kennett's biography was written by Canon Garry Bennett whose soporific sermon on another incumbent, Thomas Bray was preached before a patient Queen Elizabeth II in St Botolph's on 6 March 1980. Thomas Bray was Rector 1708-1722 and had a great interest in the world wide church, founding the Society for the Propagation of the Gospel in 1701 (now USPG) and the Society for Promoting Christian Knowledge, SPCK in 1698. The unveiling of the plaque by HM the Queen to his memory – designed and executed by David Kindersley – was a great occasion attended by the Lord Mayor and many bishops and local worthies. Among the latter was Nellie Ellis, the 90 year old flower seller in Petticoat Lane who made a splendid entry during the sermon, through the police cordon and into the gallery brandishing her reserved ticket. She sat herself amongst the choir and leaned over the balcony to get a better view of the Royal guest. Afterwards at the reception in the school hall the Queen asked me who she was so I explained that Nellie had been selling flower buttonholes on Liverpool Street before the First World War and had been at the Siege of Sydney Street. Later, against all the rules of etiquette, Nellie presented herself to the Queen with a deep curtsey saying 'I'm Nellie Ellis.' Her Majesty replied 'I know you are' and had a long talk. The church possesses a fine photograph of the famous meeting. The Royal visit had been slightly marred by a demonstration of City Polytechnic students outside the church. The Queen arrived looking like thunder, thinking they were Anti-

Royalists. I had to explain that they were protesting about Sir Keith Joseph's cuts in education budgets and HM's face, till then reminiscent of Queen Mary, relaxed.

Benjamin Pratt, curate 1699-1715 is commemorated by a plaque in the church. He purchased the patronage of the Living of Greensted near Ongar in Essex and gave it to the Bishop of London to be held for the assistant curates of Aldgate. The Bishop was bound to offer it to the curate if he was 'unmarried and sober'. Several men were preferred to Greensted because of this and Mr Marr, Rector of Aldgate 1899-1939 is buried there. Not all the Aldgate curates were a success in Greensted. Dr Andrew Hatt, who went there in 1826 is described as a 'most inferior minister', of very intemperate habits and cursed with a ferocious temper. When dining with any of his parishoners it was his custom to slip as much food as possible into his capacious pockets. One day having appropriated a chicken, a fellow guest put the sauce bowl into the pocket after it. The lady who had waited thirty years to marry him eventually did so at Greensted but then ran off soon after. When a neighbour asked to borrow a horse Mrs Hatt said 'There are two things one should never lend, a horse and a wife' to which the cleric replied 'No one will ever ask to borrow you, my dear.' After his wedding his first sermon was on the text 'My punishment is greater than I can bear'.

The City streets were by now very congested and although many houses had been rebuilt after the 1666 fire the population was still large. Four thousand one hundred families were resident in the parish and in 1710 Sir John Cass founded his school for ninety poor children at the church gate. There had in fact been a school founded in Aldgate in 1689 by voluntary contributions which must have been one of the earliest such institutions in the country.

At the beginning of the eighteenth century the church was rather dilapidated. It stood east-west 78 ft by 51 ft with galleries around three sides and it possessed six bells in its Lantern tower. Over and into the street on a wooden arm was a clock dial 'for the use of passengers.' Aldgate was an important centre for coaches. On 8 October 1740 Mr Churchwarden Watts expressed his alarm at the state of the building and it was agreed to ask the City Surveyor, Mr Dance, to look at it. Unlike most surveyors and architects Mr Dance produced a Report in twelve days. He recommended the building come down and be rebuilt. After much local debate this was agreed and even more surprisingly an Act of Parliament was speedily passed the following year to enable it to happen. The trustees were authorised to levy a rate from the local landlords and occupiers and permission was given to sell the materials of the old church. Graves and vaults were not to be disturbed and the organ was to be stored in a parishioner's house. The new church was built north-south (a sign someone said of the Protestant times) at a cost of £5,536. 2s. 5d. George Dance who designed the Mansion House, was the architect.

There appears never to have been a parsonage house, although one was rented briefly in Devonshire Square, Bishopsgate. A house was purchased in the Crescent at the southern edge of the Minories in the 1890s but this was sold in the 1930s. My predecessor, Derek Harbord, bought a house in Purley from the proceeds of the sale of the churchyard in 1966 but I decided not to live so far away from the parish so it was sold in 1984. Now a Rectory has been purchased in Shadwell.

At the rebuilding of the church there was a chance for the parish to buy the impropriation of the Living for £14,000 or for a perpetual annuity of 500 guineas per year. From earliest times tithes or a tenth part of all the produce of lands was paid to the parish church and this paid the clergy, kept the building in good order and made money available for the care of the poor. After the dissolution of the monasteries many of their beneficies including presumably St Botolph's, were impropriated or assigned to lay people called lay rectors who collected and kept the tithes although they did have to pay the clergy and keep the chancel in repair. If the Parish could raise the requested purchase price all future tithes would go not to Mr Kynaston the lay impropriator but to the church vestry who would also have the right to appoint incumbents and lecturers. After some debate the vestry felt it could only offer £13,000 and this was refused. Mr Atkinson in his 1898 history laments that such a good opportunity was lost saying at the time of his writing the parish paid £6,500 per annum to the lay impropriator funded presumably by tithes paid by rate payers. The patronage of the Living, however, passed in 1859 to the Bishop of London where it still resides. Strangely enough of all the parish churches in the City the Bishop only has this one in his patronage.

Jeremy Bentham, the famous founder of the Godless Institution of Gower Street (University College London) was baptised in St Botolph's on 15th February, 1748. His father Jeremiah was a great Aldgate worthy living at the time in Church Lane, Houndsditch. He was a wealthy lawyer and an original Trustee of the Sir John Cass's Foundation. He gave the Foundation the very beautiful silver Loving Cup which is still used each Founders Day to pledge Cass's memory. Jeremy's life was full and eventful. He devoted many years to studying constitutional law and philosophy. Reform of the poor law and jury system, prison discipline, advocacy of birth control and the introduction of census returns and post office money orders are a few of his accomplishments. He died in 1832 and being an atheist his will directed that his embalmed body should be placed in a glass case and once

2 St Botolph's, late eighteenth century

Tim Mills

a year it should preside over Governors' meetings at University College. He is still to be seen there although his head has been replaced by a wax replica. The original is between his feet in a box! Bentham's wish that present generations should never forget their predecessors has been fulfilled.

At the rear of the church a tablet commemorates William Symington (1763-1831) who constructed the first steam ship. He died in penury, was buried in the churchyard and was not remembered until the Lord Mayor in 1902 decided to commemorate the launching of the Charlotte Dundas. In association with Lord Dundas, Symington had built a steamboat with a double-acting horizontal engine and sailed her on the Forth of Clyde Canal. The vessel was a stern-wheeler, the prototype of paddle steamers. Unfortunately, just when his boat had achieved mechanical success two of the backers died and the project was abandoned. He died at his son-in-law's house near St Katharine's Dock which accounts for his burial in Aldgate.

The parish of St Botolph always possessed two parts – the Freedom part in the City and the Lordship part towards the river and by East Smithfield. In 1864 against the wishes of its 3,000 inhabitants the Lordship part was given to the new 'consolidated district' in Whitechapel. This snapped a unique historical link although the Rector is still an ex officio governor of the Aldgate Lordship Foundation.

In 1891 the Revd RH Hadden accepted the Living. He had been a curate first at St George in the East then of the Revd 'Hang Theology' Rogers of St Botolph Bishopsgate. The change from one St Botolph's to another, he said, was as from light to darkness. The exterior of the building did not inspire and the interior was bare and barn like. Two upper galleries (above the present galleries) on each side of the organ housed the children from the two local schools, their heads almost touching the ceiling. The heating was useless, windows were broken, the bells unsafe and the churchyard a receptacle for all the neighbourhood filth.

Yet Aldgate had the richest charities possible – £10,000 per annum of which £8,000 was administered by the Cass Foundation for education. Hadden castigated the Governors for lack of action. There were four voluntary schools in four separate buildings with no playgrounds at all.

In 1891 an Act of Parliament amalgamated all church charities in the Square Mile to form the City Parochial Foundation. Five parishes including St Botolph's did not join the scheme, keeping their own charity monies. When I came to St Botolph's I discovered that despite its name the City Parochial Foundation could not contribute towards our repair bills because we were outside their remit nor could they give us money for the work amongst the homeless as the secular part of the Foundation's Instrument of Government rightly forbade it helping ecclesiastical projects. They should be helped by the 'religious part.' I went to see Frank Harvey the new Archdeacon of London and he promised to try and get us back into the Scheme which he did in 1986 when he persuaded the CPF to admit St Botolph's which now receives generous grants for the fabric of the church.

Thirty separate Trusts were amalgamated in 1891 into the new Aldgate Freedom Foundation which now has thirteen governors, the Rector and Wardens being ex-officio. Bread, coal, tickets and handouts made way for 50 pensions which are paid to needy parishioners. Today the charity has a capital of approximately £500,000 which includes the freehold of the Drum and Monkey pub in Croydon and it awards pensions to people in Petticoat Square, gives a generous grant of £14,000 per annum to the crypt centre and other donations to local hospitals. For around 25 years the Cass Foundation administered the charity but now the governors have appointed their own clerk.

Mr Hadden must have been a man of great vigour for in the face of much opposition he decided the church building must be beautified but not changed out of all recognition (by for example adding a chancel as some wished). He employed JF Bentley who designed Westminster Cathedral. He suggested the galleries should be retained but pierced with a new light open balustrade, new pews were to be installed and the present ceiling with its splendid angels was to be added.

Opposition to all these changes meant that Mr Hadden had to assert his rights as incumbent. A move to elect another chairman of the vestry was defeated and he records that at the Easter Vestry in 1890 he sat in the chair for four hours protected by two stalwart members. In the end a free fight ensued and the police had to be called. Thirteen times the affairs of the parish came before the secular courts but each time he was victorious and 'the leader of the opposition was mulct in very heavy costs'.

We get an idea of who came to St Botolph's in 1891 from an interesting piece of research undertaken by Giles Enders and Ivy Walker. Looking at the Parish Register for 1891 they discovered 66 babies were baptised between January and November. Over half of the parents were not resident in the parish, but coming from the tiny streets circling the parish and places like Wapping, Walworth, Edmonton and Bow. The most numerous professions of the fathers are clerk, policeman and labourer but there are also housekeepers, hosiers, lightermen, valets, cabinet-makers, porters, mariners and carpenters.

The parishes of St Botolph and Holy Trinity Minories were united on January 1 1899. £150 of Holy Trinity's income was assigned to St Botolph's for a curate and other income was given to St Mary, Bow. This may explain why in 1976 Prebendary Arthur Royall the then Rector of Bow discovered a 1637 chalice, 1719 paten and 1808 alms dish belonging to Holy Trinity in the safe of his church. He kindly returned them to me at St Botolph's.

The first incumbent of the united parish was the Revd James Marr who stayed for forty years and was also for 18 years Chairman of the Cass Foundation. He was one of those responsible for the new building which still houses the Cass Primary School, and was Area Dean of East City 1916-35. When he came to Aldgate it was a parish of small houses and narrow lanes, alleys and courts. When he died in 1938, large office blocks had been built standing beside warehouses and shops. He possessed great pastoral gifts fortunately linked with a flair for administration – very necessary in a post which involved and still involves much committee work. He was able to help set up the Cass Institute where technical training was given on all subjects from metal work to brewing. His Memorial Service was held in a packed church and the sermon was given by the Archdeacon of London which is surprising because the Bishop, Winnington Ingram, had been in office for almost exactly the same time as Mr Marr. Strange, too, that he was not given a prebendal stall in St Paul's, despite being the City's senior incumbent.

A pleasant modern link with him for me has been my friendship with his daughter Margaret whom I met at the Royal Foundation of Saint Katharine in 1980 and she then maintained a strong interest in St Botolph's. She remembered going to Bishop Winnington Ingram's Christmas parties which were held before the first world war in his house in St James' Square. Horse drawn brakes would leave different parts of the diocese and converge on central London. One would leave Bow and collect the Stepney and City incumbents' children all of whom had a marvellous time eating quantities of food and racing round the huge house with the bachelor bishop arranging the games. She died in 1993 leaving a generous bequest to the Church.

During the 1939-45 war the then Rector, the Revd JPR Rees Jones, slept in the crypt and fire watched during air raids with his volunteers. Some damage was done in the raid of 8 October 1941 which meant the weather vane was removed from the tower and the highest stage of the steeple removed. A bomb fell through the roof on to the gallery but fortunately did not explode. Another fragment missed the organ console by inches but destroyed the pedal board. A secondhand one was quickly found.

The ravages of war took their toll some twenty years later when on a stormy night in 1957 a fragment of masony crashed down from the tower.

An inspection revealed the original iron bands round the tower were rusting through so a general restoration of the outside of the building was undertaken at a cost of £12,000. George Appleton became Rector in January 1957 and he records in his autobiography *Unfinished* that at his interview the wardens asked how he would spend his time as nearly all the parishioners were Jews. 'With a feeling of rash abandon' he said he would like to make St Botolph's a centre for new relationships 'Not with Jews only but with Buddhists, Hindus and Muslims as well.' The wardens were enthusiastic and he got the job. Once again the lack of a Rectory caused problems but Basil Jansz, Vicar of Shadwell and a friend of George, invited him and Marjorie to move into a flat in his Vicarage. George received as I did in 1974 a warm welcome from Norman Motley at St Michael Cornhill who had founded the Othona Community in Essex as a place for conferences and retreats. He also was welcomed by Tubby Clayton of All Hallows by the Tower, the Founder of Toc H (whom I ministered to in the London Hospital shortly before his death) and later by Father Joe Williamson whose great work was amongst the prostitutes of Cable Street. The four musketeers as George called them met regularly for worship, discussion and companionship.

George formed a close and very special link with his Jewish parishioners. So much so that he is remembered with great affection today thirty-five years later. Without conditions or sinister evangelistic motives he made friends and people appreciated that and used him as a spiritual counsellor and guide. St Botolph's was by now – as it still is – the centre of the London Diocesan Council for Christian-Jewish Understanding and an annual lecture was held in St Paul's Cathedral given in alternate years by Jewish and Christian scholars. The lecture is still held but now takes place in St Botolph's.

It was Appleton who started the work amongst the homeless. He enlisted the help of the Ward Alderman, Bernard Waley-Cohen, who fortunately was Lord Mayor 1961-62 and was thus able to help get some money for the new plans. After a while the social worker, Harry King talked with George about the number of young people roaming the streets and a club for them was opened in the western tunnel of the crypt. Friends provided the necessary furniture, fridge and cooker. About fifty teenagers arrived each day and no formal programme was prepared. The juke box provided a focus for the dancing and the only rules were no drinking, drugs or flick knives.

The World Congress of Faiths, probably because of George's known views and the warmth of his hospitality, asked if their annual service could be in St Botolph's. Remembering his conversation with the churchwardens he asked them if they would accept the challenge – no Anglican church had ever hosted the service. They agreed. 'I wanted the service to be one of real fellowship but also one of real religious integrity with no blurring of differences and with no singing of hymns so vague in their content that anyone might sing them and I wanted the prayer to be such as people of each faith could pray in their own way within the silence of their own hearts.' The Service thus had no set prayers, no hymns but biddings of worship together with readings from the various scriptures.

The Bishop of Stepney, Everard Lunt agreed that George should have the help of a licensed lay worker so moved Trudie Eulenburg from St George in the East where amongst her other duties she had to stoke the boiler each morning! 'She's not everyone's cup of tea' said the Bishop, 'but she is quite clearly a very good brand of her own.' She enthusiastically threw herself into the two crypt clubs and was still helping them both in a very practical way when I arrived. For many years she cared for her distinguished father until he died aged 103 and she somehow managed to combine this with her duties upstairs and downstairs as parish worker or as one of the Petticoat Lane traders called her 'The Rector's woman.' She retired in December, 1984 but still helps out in the church.

George went on later to be Archbishop of Jerusalem from where he retired. Countless people use his books of prayers and read his articles in the Press. Sadly his wife Marjorie died in 1980 in Oxford. George says 'Every night before going to sleep I try to tell her of the happenings of the past day, good and not so good. I know that before long I shall make my final migration and join her.' He himself died in 1993.

Derek Harbord, formerly the Hon Mr Justice Harbord, one of Her Majesty's High Court Judges Overseas, succeeded George in 1962. An astute man blessed with an acidic wit and terse turn of phrase, he was already aged sixty when he became Rector. In his twenties he was called to the Bar and then ordained into the Anglican Church in 1925. He served in several parishes but in 1935 resigned as vicar of the Good Shepherd, West Bromwich to become a Roman Catholic and practise at the English Bar. After a spell at the Old Bailey he joined the colonial Legal Service and went as a district magistrate and coroner in the Gold Coast. From 1953 to 1959 he was a Judge of the High Court of Tanganyika and told me several times how much he enjoyed having his own train to travel to the remoter districts. He returned to Ghana as an academic and there he was reconciled to the Church of England through his friendship with the Bishop of Accra. His entry in *Who's Who* listed his recreations as 'keeping trace of 26 grand and great grandchildren, reading modern theology and other who dunnits. Pottering about.'

Derek Harbord continued the work in the crypt but his time at St Botolph's was more concerned with buildings and administration than people. He would have made a first rate Archdeacon. In fact his talents were just those needed. At a sermon preached at the end of his incumbency he told the congregation, 'I have been a deacon, now you need a priest.' When I was appointed I went trembling and shaking to dine with him at the Athenaeum. He was a most gentle, gracious witty host and I enjoyed every minute of our various meetings. His letters to me always began 'My dear Tight-Rope Walker'.

On 19 August 1965 at 4.30 p.m. a fire broke out in the sacristy of the Church. Its cause has never been established although Harbord suspected arson. All the vestments, altar frontals and communion vessels were destroyed, together with various wall plaques in the sacristy. The intense heat blistered the paint in the rest of the church and some of the ceiling plaster came down. Two of the three Victorian reredos panels were destroyed and the woodwork round the altar was damaged. The Fire Brigade arrived promptly so by the evening the main church was a blackened, soggy mess. Fortunately the roof and galleries remained but a Dangerous Structure Notice was served

In his letter to the Bishop (Robert Stopford, an old friend) the next day the Rector stressed 'business as usual' and suggested services be held in the crypt. This was agreed. The baptism fixed for the following Sunday took place in the Three Nuns Tavern where the family lodged. The next day's Holy Communion was taken by Mr Harbord in a suit. 'I hope you don't disapprove of this' he said to the Bishop then added 'I telephoned your number and that of the Archdeacon last evening in order to appraise you of this happening without delay but could get no reply'. Things do not change.

It may have looked a little suspicious that the building insurance had been increased from £30,000 to £200,000 shortly before the fire. The Ecclesiastical Insurance Office Ltd however paid up, and on the afternoon of Tuesday 8 November 1966 HM Queen Elizabeth the Queen Mother attended a Service of Re-hallowing and Thanksgiving. The Lord Mayor wearing his state robes and the Bishop of London took part in the proceedings, which began with the Bishop enquiring in Harbordese 'Father Rector, for what purpose have you requested our presence here today?' There was certainly much to be thankful for. Had the Fire Brigade arrived any later the building would have been completely destroyed. Alderman Sir Bernard Waley-Cohen had raised £5,000 to restore the bells and install an electrical system to function when there were no ringers available; the beauty of the interior was greatly enhanced by the plans of the architect Rodney Tatchell whose father like him was architect to St Botolph's for 26 years. He retired in 1981 and John Phillips took over. New glass doors engraved by June Armstrong meant the thousands of passers by could now look into the church. The lettering says 'A House of Prayer for all nations. Pray for all who travel by land, air or water.'

Two large stone tablets were fixed in the narthex by the font listing the Rectors and Aldermen. The new windows in the church contained the coats of arms of eleven Portsoken Ward Aldermen who were Lord Mayor of London. Amongst them are those of Sir Bernard who delighted in telling everyone he was the only living Jew who had a window all to himself in an Anglican church.

Two other important matters taxed Harbord's administrative gifts. The City Corporation compulsorily purchased a large slice of churchyard to build a road to the north of the church. At first only £14,500 was offered for the 3,500 sq. ft. but in the end thanks to the tenacity and negotiating skills of Fred Hippolite of the chuch surveyors Biscoe and Stanton a total of £137,500 was received. Amongst other things this bought the Rectory in Purley, endowed the Living, paid for necessary repairs to the church and created a capital sum which would provide the PCC with an annual income.

The redevelopment of the Three Nuns site to the east of the church (now the site of Eagle Star Ltd) presented further problems. Planning permission for a shelter in the churchyard and the urinal ('clochemerle' in all Harbord's correspondence) had been given for a limited time and there was some worry that the new arrangement would interfere with the work of the crypt. In the event, thanks to a give and take of land, a new boundary wall was erected. At the time the application was made by the developers there was no obligation to advertise the proposals. Considering how high handed the Corporation and the developers were we are lucky to have a decent outlook to the east. In 1989 Eagle Star informed me they would be demolishing their building. I expressed surprise as only fifteen years earlier I had been driven out of my mind by the noise of constructing the present building. The recession has, however, postponed the plans.

The youth work continued in Derek Harbord's incumbency. Membership aged 14-21 was around 200 and on six nights a week up to 170 young people crowded in for coffee, table tennis and a chat. The school gym was used for boxing and badminton. A hand bell team was formed and two City Police cadets helped form a band. Camping, hiking and mountaineering were summer pursuits. 'On the whole', said Derek 'members dislike being organised and *run* as much as would members of the Athenaeum and we make a point of respecting their independence.'

Mr Harry King remained as a salaried full-time leader helped by a part-time leader. A sixpence admission charge and a generous grant from the LCC meant the books could be balanced.

After a while the focus of the centre was on the local Asian boys and girls in Whitechapel and Spitalfields who had no club of their own. They were willing to come across the complicated road system to Aldgate and the City and Tower Hamlets Youth Office funded a full-time youth worker, Dr Ahmed. I owed a lot to Harold Finch the Borough Youth Officer who advised me on my arrival at Aldgate about this club. Soon it became apparent that local clubs were starting up in the Brick Lane area and our membership dwindled. At the same time the Wayholme Project centred on Trinity Square had revealed the problem of homelessness amongst East End young people. Linda Watts, their researcher created a network of local people concerned at this problem including Ken Leech, Marybel Moore, John Newbiggin, David Randall, Dan Jones and myself. I agreed to be the chairman of a new project called 'Kipper' for young people kipping on the streets and the project moved into the crypt. Josie Harriott, from Wapping, larger than life, was a trained youth worker and soon made contact with many youngsters at risk. A hostel was set up in White Horse Lane, Stepney and later it moved to its present location in Bow Road.

David Randall, now the Director and founder of CARA which cares for those living with the HIV virus, stayed nearly three years at St Botolph's as a youth chaplain then became Vicar of St Clement Notting Dale. Bishop Gerald maintained an interest in the work and agreed to spend an evening going round the East End clubs incognito which to him meant laying aside his purple and donning a smart country suit and tie. He looked like the local squire and seemed pleased to be introduced by David as 'my friend Gerald.' Win Noonan at the Still and Star gave the tour a flying start by providing the Bishop with a very large double brandy at the bar.

David made contact with all sorts of people and was greatly helped by Derek Cox whose work at Avenues Unlimited showed him what could be done. When David left the staff in 1977 we had to decide whether to continue the youth work but due to lack of space we decided to put all our energies into work amongst the homeless. I was sorry to see David leave as he has so many gifts and talents and resembled the old style East End priest who was not afraid to play the piano in the pub. The Services he held in St Botolph's on various themes like 'Christ the Clown' or 'Christ the Healer' drew a large crowd and were very popular. David's work in the AIDS field has been a real inspiration to many of us and, as ever, he meets and helps countless people who have no contact with any of the churches.

3 MONASTIC ALDGATE

Aldgate was a very religious place in Medieval England. The Priory of Holy Trinity stood just inside the old or ald gate to the west and the convent of St Clare stood to the south of the gate. It seems remarkable that two such large Religious houses were so close to one another.

Holy Trinity Priory

In 1107 an Augustinian Canon called Norman opened a religious house at the Aldgate end of Leadenhall Street. Queen Maud or Matilda, wife of Henry I and daughter-in-law of William the Conqueror was much charmed by Prior Norman's eloquence and made him her confessor. She was thinking of founding a monastic house and prompted by Archbishop Anselm and Bishop Richard Beaumers of London she gave Norman a parcel of land just inside the ald gate. The Queen's Charter is still extant and in it we read that she gave a mill on the River Lea to the Abbey of Waltham in exchange for a tiny piece of land which was now incorporated into the new monastery called Holy Trinity and afterwards Christ Church. Its architecture and size resembled the present Southwark Cathedral and it became the richest conventual house in England and certainly one of the largest. It extended from Creechchurch Lane to Dukes Place and north to Heneage Lane. Spacious cloisters led into a huge church and we are told that the ceremonial was of the most splendid kind and the singing and chanting such that parishioners and travellers 'rejoiced mightily at it'.

The Priory was immensely wealthy as Matilda gave it endowments which included two thirds of the income from the City of Exeter together with the control of Aldgate one of the seven entrances to the City. In 1291 the Priory received income from 72 London parishes and in 1125 the Knighten Guild surrendered the land outside the ald gate to Prior Norman who laid the title deeds on the altar. The monastery with its eight altars must have been very grand indeed because on 8 April 1244 Fulk Bassett was consecrated Bishop of London there. In 1256 the monks blotted their copy book by sheltering a thief who had escaped from Newgate so the King – Henry III – temporarily took the Priory into his own hands. Having control over the lands of Portsoken Ward and its church of St Botolph meant that the Prior had great power. However, he met his match in 1255 when the King's wife, Eleanor quarrelled with him over her religious house, St Katharine's by the Tower.

In 1148 Queen Matilda, wife of King Stephen obtained some land near the Tower by the River Thames from the Prior of Holy Trinity who was also Rector of St Botolph's. On it she founded the Hospital of St Katharine for a Master, Brothers and Sisters and other poor persons. The rent charged to the Queen was £6 per year. She asked the monks to have custody of St Katharine's but reserved to herself and future Queens the nomination of Master and this arrangement continued until 1255 when Queen Eleanor brought a suit against the Prior claiming he was mismanaging the Hospital. Not surprisingly the Lord Mayor and Aldermen backed the Alderman Prior's claim to be in charge of St Katharine's so the Queen wrote to the Bishop of London saying the Hospital was now 'destitute of all discipline and the goods thereof wasted by the Prior'. Her letters, she said, went unanswered. The Bishop visited St Katharine's on St Giles' Day 1257 when the Prior and his brethren told him they had a temporal right over the Hospital by legal contract and a spiritual right as the land was in the parish of St Botolph's. The Bishop asked why one of the Holy Trinity brothers was Master, to which the response was that the St Katharine's brothers used to get drunk every day so needed someone to control them. The Bishop, presumably bowing to Royal Authority, removed the Master and inhibited the monks from meddling in the Hospital's affairs. He appointed a new Master, Gilbert. The next Bishop, Henry de Wyngeham, ordered the Prior and Brothers to appear before him and after much altercation told them to give up their claim to St Katharine's or they would incur the King's displeasure. The Pope tried unsuccessfully to get the situation changed but control passed to the Queen Consort where it still remains.

Not having much choice the Prior/Rector of Aldgate gave up his control and 'became generously inclined' and granted the lease of the land of the churchyard at St Katharine's on condition that two pounds of wax should be delivered to him 'at the day of St Botolph'. Because of this close link between St Botolph's and St Katharine's I was very honoured to be appointed Master of The Royal Foundation by Queen Elizabeth the Queen Mother who takes a very keen interest in the Foundation's affairs and visits it regularly.

Discipline in Holy Trinity left a lot to be desired and in 1303 the Archbishop of Canterbury tried to enforce stricter rules. Apparently the younger brothers or Canons were going astray in the London streets so they were told in future they must be accompanied by an older brother. Women were now to be excluded from the holiest parts of the building 'unless they were women of good fame passing through on a pilgrimage in which case they must leave as soon as devotions are over.' In 1493, scandal occured again when Bishop Hill of London discovered that Prior Thomas Percy was forcing his colleagues to describe a Mrs Joan Hodgis as an embroidress to the Priory 'in order to facilitate intercourse'.

The Prior reigned over both the Priory and the parish as a temporal and spiritual leader. The first Common Council meeting of the City was held in 1347, the Prior/Alderman being present together with six councillors from Portsoken, Peter de Weston, John de Romeneys, Alexander Cobbe, Alexander Mareschal, John de Louge and Thomas de Caxtone. The number rose to eight in the twelfth century but today with a much reduced population it has four common councillors – Roger Brighton, Geoffrey Lawson Alfred Dunitz and Iris Samuel, deputy to the Alderman.

King Henry VIII ordered the Priory to be dissolved and all the vestments and ecclesiastical furniture were removed to St Botolph's on 4 February 1531. The King made the last Prior Nicholas Hancock ask for dissolution as the House was in debt. Apparently he was frightened to leave the premises for fear of arrest over an outstanding £11 butcher's bill. The King gave the Priory, its plate and lands to Sir Thomas Audley to whom he owed a favour and so it became the first monastic house to be given to a layman. Sir Thomas (afterwards Lord Audley of Walden) Speaker of the House of Commons became Lord Chancellor and died at Aldgate in 1554. To him fell the sorry task of pulling down the great church. The stone was taken away for seven pence a cartload although much was used to build Sir Thomas a great house. Four of the bells were sold to Stepney and five smaller ones to St Stephen's, Coleman Street and some stones were used to build local houses but no traces of these survive.

With the proceeds of the sale of Holy Trinity a great house was built at Audley End near Saffron Walden. Sir Thomas's daughter, Margaret, married Thomas Duke of Norfolk and the City house and land passed to him in 1554. He was beheaded in 1573, and is commemorated by 'Dukes Place'.

Now nothing remains of the powerful and wealthy Holy Trinity except an arch and wall dating from the twelfth and fifteenth centuries which is still to be found inside Swiss Re house on the corner of Leadenhall and Mitre streets. The Museum of London who recently made a detailed study of the area suggest that the arch connected the south choir of the church with a side chapel. Close to here, in 1137, two of King Stephen's young children, Baldwin and Matilda, were buried on either side of the high altar of the Priory. Visitors are invited into the vestibule of Swiss Re house to view the arch and a small exhibition.

Abbey of St Clare, Minories

Minories takes its name from the nuns of the Abbey – the Poor Clares, the Minoresses. St Francis founded a First Order for men and a Second Order for women. The convent of the Sorores Minores was founded here in 1293 by Blanche the wife of Edmund Earl of Lancaster. Earlier she had been married to the King of Navarre and when he died she kept her royal title. Queen Blanche's great granddaughter married John of Gaunt, mother of Henry IV so Blanche is an ancestress of our Royal Family. Various endowments of land and privileges were granted to the Sisters over the years so they were not exactly impoverished. However, except for pestilence, war or famine they were forbidden to leave their convent .

The land on which the Abbey was built was in fact a Roman burial ground. It occupied land to the east of Minories between the present bus station and Portsoken Street. When the present office block at the east end of St Clare Street was built in 1983 over 2,000 pottery shards, mostly Roman, were discovered together with pots, beakers and animal bones. A coin of Domitian (AD 81-86) was found beside a skull. Romans buried their dead outside the city walls and the area of the present Saint Clare Street was probably used as a cemetery for 300 years. One pit contained skeletons of a heron, mice, voles and 82 frogs. This was presumably a ritual burial pit of some description but nothing similar has so far been found elsewhere. At an adjoining site in 1853 a Roman sarcophagus (3-4 century) was found and this is now in the British Museum.

Edmund (brother of Edward Ist) and Blanche brought the Franciscan Sisters from France in 1293 and lost no time in building the Abbey in the Parish of St Botolph's. The precincts covered five acres. Many ladies of rank joined the Order presumably bringing with them land and money. Thirteen Abbesses are recorded between 1294 and 1538. The sisters wore a gown of grey wool, a white coif on the head covered by a black veil. It is recorded that 27 of the nuns died from the plague in 1515. Many distinguished people were buried in the Abbey. Edmund the founder was interred in Westminster abbey but his heart was placed near the convent altar. Anne Mowbray, a daughter of the Duke of Norfolk who at the age of seven married the second son of King Edward IV (one of the Princes murdered in the Tower) died in 1481. In 1963 when an office building was erected on the site her coffin was discovered and reburied in Westminster Abbey. I have a letter written by my distinguished predecessor in his best biting legal language to the Home Office regretting that the Rector of the Parish was not informed before the reburial took place.

Under Henry VIII religious houses were dissolved and their lands reverted to the Crown. The last Abbess, Lady Elizabeth Savage resigned and received a pension of £40 per year. The 24 other nuns aged 16 to 76 were not so fortunate and received only sums between one and four pounds a year. However this was more generous than pensions awarded at the other Religious Houses. The convent chapel now became a church for the local inhabitants and soon a separate parish of Holy Trinity Minories was carved out of St Botolph's. The new parish was tiny, no more that 255 ft in length. The Bishop of London had no authority over it until 1730. The parish which only covered the site of the convent precincts had its outline area unnaturally excluded from the City. It is now in the Borough of Tower Hamlets but the City are soon to annex it.

The other Convent buildings remained empty for two years and were then granted to the Bishop of Bath and Wells as his London residence. His successor exchanged the land for other property and in 1552 the young King Edward VI, son of Henry, granted it to Henry Grey Duke of Suffolk the father of Lady Jane Grey who on Edward's death was proclaimed Queen on 10 July 1553 and was deposed nine days later. She, her husband and her father were beheaded.

In 1852 a head embedded in a thick mass of sawdust which had preserved it was found in one of the vaults beneath Holy Trinity Church. The hair and beard fell off and word went around that is belonged to the unfortunate Duke of Suffolk. Experts from the National Portrait Gallery thought it looked like the painting in their care but a surgeon from the London Hospital pointed out it had not been cleanly cut by an axe but hacked off the body probably with a small knife. The Revd E M Tomlinson, Vicar of Holy Trinity, placed it in a glass case which resided in St Botolph's sacristy for some years. George Appleton used to refer to it as 'one of the amenities of Aldgate'. In 1974 I was asked by a man accompanied by his young son if he might view The Head. I had no idea what he was talking about but discovered that my predecessor, so revolted by the head-in-a-box glaring at him as he vested for divine Service had buried it beneath the church's front steps. We found it there in 1984 when we extended the south vault and I interred it in the west tunnel of the crypt where we were strengthening the floor by putting concrete around the coffins beneath.

The mummified head found in the Minories is almost certainly not the head of the Duke of Suffolk. More likely the body was a casualty of rather unsavoury happenings in 1786 when the beadle Mr Smallcole was caught in the crypt sawing up the coffin wood to make floor boards for his house or for firewood.

John Stow the historian wrote in 1598 that there were large stone houses for 'armour and habilments of war' near the church and a farm where he bought milk and in the summer three pints of ale for a halfpenny. Mr Trolop then Mr Goodman were the farmers there. Goodman's son, says Stow, let out the ground for grazing horses and garden plots 'and lived like a gentleman thereby'. His name is remembered today in Goodman's Yard and Goodman Street.

After the Dissolution the Abbey grounds with its church reverted to the Crown and was used largely as a munitions store for the Ordnance Office. The great Mansion House was utilised as the principal store whilst other buildings became workshops and residences for the various officials. In 1564 Edward Randolph was appointed Lieutenant-General of the Ordnance to be in charge of the land 'without the gate of Aldgate'.

During the Civil War the Parliamentarians took possession of the Minories, The Tower and the Store Houses. A Great Workhouse belonging to the City corporation was set up. This only lasted a few years as at the Restoration Charles II appointed Colonel William Legge as Lieutenant General and the Workhouse was closed. St Botolph's still possesses a fine pair of silver flagons presented by him to Holy Trinity Church in 1669. Legge, a loyal servant of the Crown during the Civil War had married the daughter of Sir William Washington a forbear of George Washington. He is the ancestor of the present Lord Dartmouth who in 1975 brought me the breast plates of lead, silver, copper and brass taken from the coffins of the members of the family in the Dartmouth vault, the contents of which were removed when the site was deconsecrated in 1950. Colonel Legge died at Minories House on 13 October 1672 aged 83 and was buried beneath the chancel of the church. An impressive monument was erected and on it appeared his coat of arms incorporating the Washington stars and stripes which were used for the American national flag. William Legge's son became the first Lord Dartmouth. Charles II now granted the Abbey known as Mansion House to Sir Thomas Chicheley Master of the Ordnance but he sold it to Sir William Pritchard who was Lord Mayor in 1683 and resided in Mansion House, Minories. It is almost certain that this name was thereafter used for the official residence of the Lord Mayor. The present Mansion House built in 1738 was designed by George Dance who also designed St Botolph's.

Fortunately Holy Trinity escaped the Great Fire but in 1706 it was so dilapidated it was rebuilt. The north wall, however, was left and it was this wall which was revealed in 1904 when the next door railway warehouse was demolished. Two bricked up windows and a doorway – which had presumably led to the Abbey garden- were revealed.

The rebuilding in 1706 cost £700 and the church was panelled all round to a height of six feet. The Church possesses a small piece of this panelling which Fabian Moynihan gave to St Botolph's. He found it in an antique shop. The reredos was similar to that in the present St Botolph's which was built a few years later. The centre panel had an 18th century 'glory' surrounding a dove. Without knowing it I wanted to copy this idea when I asked John Piper to design new panels for the St Botolph's reredos. With Patrick Reyntiens, he came to see me twice and sat in the church for a while. 'I want the theme to be the Gateway of Heaven' I told him 'as we are a Gate church'. 'I don't know what heaven looks like' said Piper, 'Revelation 21 gives you a good idea of what you see looking through the gate', I ventured. Piper went off to think about it and I gather a few weeks later when he went to say farewell to the dying Benjamin Britten he told him of the awkward commission. 'Go and look at the glory behind the altar in Framlingham church', said Britten and pulled out one of his record sleeves which had used it as an illustration. Piper duly presented a design which sadly none of us liked. It was a mixture of paint and ceramic and looked somewhat like a dart board. He gave it to me and it hangs on my attic stairs, having been embarrassingly rejected by the church at Aldgate.

A famous worshipper at Holy Trinity Minories, Sir Isaac Newton 1642-1727, lived in Haydon Square (named after the Master of Ordnance, Sir William Haydon). He was Warden of the Mint and an engraving of Sir Isaac hung in the vestry.

In the latter part of the 17th century the church of Holy Trinity became a source of scandal as its incumbent agreed to marry couples without banns or licence. He claimed the parish was a Royal Peculiar as the Pope had released it from the authority of the Archbishop of Canterbury and the Bishop of London placing it under the Sovereign. The parish of Holy Trinity thus became a miniature kingdom of its own. There were many comings and goings to Fulham to see the Bishop of London and the churchwardens were imprisoned for not submitting to his authority. However, clandestine weddings continued serving the needs of those who did not want banns or licence and lining the pockets of the incumbent or clerk. Tomlinson reckons that over 32,000 marriages took place between 1644 and 1695 of which 5,600 were celebrated by Mr Weston (1679-86). The register books have been conveniently lost but we know the incumbent in a good year earnt £300, a very large sum in the seventeenth century. Sometimes in the rush the clerk forgot to ask the bride's name. 'July 19 1688 Peter Poots a solger was married ye same day but ye paper that his and her name tok on was lost'.

In 1695 an agreement was reached with the Bishop of London and numbers of weddings began to decline. In 1695 there were 477, in 1704, 109 and in 1754 an Act of Parliament put an end to it all. The incumbent then was Dr Henry Fly who reigned for 63 years till 1873 whilst at the same time being Vicar of Willesden.

The Parish began to lose many of its residents in 1770 when the East India company purchased a considerable area of land for warehouses. In 1851 the census revealed 572 parishioners were living in 65 houses. In the same year many of these were taken over by the London and Blackwall Railway Company who built large arches in Haydon Square over which the new railway would run and by the end of the century few houses remained.

In 1893 the parish was re-united with St Botolph's but the union could not take place until six years later when the Revd Samuel Kinns ceased to be incumbent. The oak pulpit of 1709 was given to East Meon church in Hampshire where it remains today.

The building then became a Parish Institute for St Botolph's but unfortunately was destroyed by enemy action on 9 September 1940. In 1959 the site was sold for a paltry sum and half was given to St Botolph's. An office building was erected and as the tiny churchyard (now the car park) is still church property the Rector has a car parking space in perpetuity. Another building was erected in 1983 which is owned by Pearl Assurance (Unit Funds) Ltd. The Church was under some pressure to sell the car park but refused. The last offer was £47,000 in 1984. A Freehold in the City is a good thing to possess and the parish gets a useful sum each year in rent.

Abbesses of the Convent of St Clare

Katerine de Ingham c1360
Edeanor Scrope c1388
Lady Mary de Lisle c1398
Lady Margaret Holmystede c1408
Isabella of Gloucester c1421
Elizabeth Horwode c1470
Johanna Barton c1481
Elizabeth Boulman c1508
Dorothy Cumberford 1514
Elizabeth Savage 1524

4 THE LOCAL AREA AND ITS VILLAINS

Standing on the steps of St Botolph's one looks westwards to see all the wealth of the City of London. Banks and business houses, despite the recession give an impression of financial confidence. To the east however, lies Tower Hamlets, always an area of deprivation, where over the years public schools, universities and other benefactors have arrived to do good works. Today St Botolph's still has a Robin Hood ministry, helping the wealthy City face up to the problems of homelessness. Chaim Bermant in his *Point of Arrival* says that the East End has always served the metropolis. 'Here with its vast warehouses flanking the river like a prison wall were the great docks which fed London and stored the merchandise which supplied its wealth . . . Here were the bakeries and sugar refineries, the breweries – Mann's, Charrington's, etc – and Bryant & May's matchworks. Here were hand loom weavers of Spitalfields . . . the shoemakers who shod it . . . and the Jewish garment workers who clothed it. The East End lived on London but London lived on the East End.'

The East End had its pockets of wealth even in the nineteenth century but reading the Victorian press the impression is one of an area stuffed full of thieves, murderers and cut-throats. Occasionally there were other oddities such as when in 1879 the End End Observer reported a drag ball held in a hall in Mansell Street. 'It appeared to be a fancy ball and although the dancers wore female attire the police officers soon discovered that there were not half a dozen women in the place. People danced together, kissed each other and behaved in anything but an orderly manner.'

The Church of England always had a tough time making an impression on the area. Charles James Blomfield, Bishop of London, built twelve churches with their attendant halls, vicarages and occasionally a gymnasium in Bethnal Green between 1828 and 1850. He named them after the twelve apostles and some have survived Hitler and the modern redundancy notices issued by the diocese. Heroic efforts were made by clergy like Lowder of London Docks, Dolling of Poplar, Jay of Shoreditch (immortalised in Arthur Morrison's *Child of the Jago*) and Barnett of Whitechapel but very few Eastenders entered church buildings, except to collect hand-outs. The same is true today. I doubt whether many Anglican churches in Tower Hamlets have a Sunday congregation of over a hundred people.

The area was certainly impoverished. In May 1887 Charles Booth presented the first findings of his research, *Life and Labour of the People of London*. In a total population of 456,877 his researchers found thirteen per cent faced daily starvation and 22 per cent lived on the poverty line which was defined as twenty-one shillings per week for a moderate sized family. Whitechapel had a much higher percentage than the rest of the area but the highest rate of deprivation (50 per cent) was in the St George's district. Whilst Booth provided the cold stark figures, novelists such as Arthur Morrison and Margaret Harkness gave a more exact description. Bill Fishman's *East End 1888* gives an excellent picture of life in that year.

From the very earliest times the River Thames carried immigrants into the heart of London and in 1551 the Lord Mayor in a survey discovered 40,000 'aliens' living in and around London, besides 'women and children for the most part heretics fled from other countries.' Huguenots, the largest group, began to arrive at this time but after the revocation of the Edict of Nantes in 1685 over 100,000 fled from France and settled here. They were welcomed because they brought with them many skills and talents. Amongst which was silk weaving and soon the brocades, damasks and velvets of Spitalfields were famous and sought after. By 1775 Spitalfields had lost its fields and gardens and began to be over-crowded. Still today one can get a flavour of that period by walking around Elder and Fournier Streets and their environs. In the eighteenth century there were sixteen Huguenot churches in and around Spitalfields serving some 15,000 people who lived amongst the local people there. Unfortunately, due to a number of causes business decreased and in the early 19th century the spread of the power loom meant wages fell to starvation level and national appeals for help were launched by the Bishop of London and others. Soon trade ceased completely but the Huguenots remained living in poverty. Spitalfields became an area of squalor. L'Eglise Neuve built in 1743 in Brick Lane became a synagogue.

The Irish also arrived. Many of those who left Ireland in the 18th and 19th centuries to escape starvation settled in Whitechapel and Spitalfields. Early in the last century there was work to be had building the docks then manning them so they worked and drank hard and were not averse to joining riots or rebellions. Of the fourteen ringleaders arrested after the 1769 riots several had Irish names. Being Catholic the Irish immigrants were treated with abuse and suspicion even after the 1828 Irish Emancipation. The older Catholic families in England showed little compassion for the immigrants and when some local priests wrote to the two-hundred titled Catholic families for donations to build a church they only received five pounds. However, the hundreds of poor Catholics supported and cared for each other and thus survived.

The Jews are perhaps the best known immigrants. Unlike the Germans who had come to work in the breweries or sugar refineries or the Chinese in Limehouse, the Jews were noticeable. Their clothing, diet, religion and way of life set them apart from their neighbours. In 1753 there were a mere 10,000 in England. Jews had been expelled from this country between 1290 and 1656 and the first to return were the prosperous Sephardim of Spanish and Portuguese origin. It was these who built the Bevis Marks Synagogue. Ashkenazim as Jews of Polish and German origin are known also began to arrive. The jobs they took were humble, tailors, cobblers, old clothes dealers but by 1850 some had acquired a good education and moved into the professions, having houses in the City or West End. The Jewish street dealers began to give way to the Irish who being on the starvation line were willing to work all hours for little return. Although the Jewish community was small by 1851 a school had been established in Bell Lane, a widows' home in Aldgate, a hospital in the Mile End Road and an orphanage in Goodmans Fields. Israel Zangwill's novel *Children of the Ghetto* describes the everyday lives of Jewish families in Aldgate and Whitechapel and the compassionate work of the Board of Guardians.

In March, 1881 Tsar Alexander II of Russia was assassinated. A period of liberal treatment of Jews was thus over and a series of anti-Jewish riots culminating in institutionalised violence from the authorities of Russia and Poland meant thousands of Jews fled abroad. The Lord Mayor set up a relief fund in London but it soon became apparent that the numbers were overwhelming. Protests were made and people were urged to travel on to America. Some thought they had arrived in America when they landed at Wapping and days went by before they realised their mistake. More immigrants flooded in after the 1903 Pogrom when the most terrible atrocities were perpetrated in Kishinev. The British Brothers League, formed to resist the 'alien invasion', held a meeting attended by 4,000 in the Peoples Palace (now the hall of Queen Mary Westfield College). Speakers used phrases loaded with hate. 'We are not the dustbin of Europe and no rubbish should be shot here' was the general theme. Violent incidents ensued when immigrants tried to move into houses. Sanitary inspectors were sent to look at their living and working conditions. One visited a house in Goulston Street where Mr and Mrs Cohen lived with two children and 139 hens. In other houses every room was occupied by an entire family. In 1902 a Royal Commission was appointed to consider the problem of immigration, Lord Rothschild being one of the members. They discovered that there were other causes to the congestion. Houses had been torn down to build factories and breweries and even the destruction of slums and the building of artisan dwellings meant only half of those living in the old tenements could now be re-housed. The Royal Commission proposed restrictions which were opposed by Winston Churchill and the Liberals. They quoted the Huguenot immigration and thought the country had benefited greatly by the skills of immigrants. The Bill based on the recommendations was carried but when the Liberals came to power they rarely enforced its clauses and in 1914 with the outbreak of war all immigration ended.

The latest wave of newcomers are different again from the predecessors, mostly coming from one district in Bangladesh. The Mezuzoth, the scrolls on the doorpost of Jewish households still remain in Petticoat Tower and Square but the residents of the other part of the parish – Guinness and Iveagh Courts, are mostly Bengali, and the Church School, Sir John Cass's Primary, is now 80 per cent Muslim. Spitalfields Church of England School has no Christians in it apart from the staff. In the sixties Kosher butchers gave way to Halal butchers and the Brick Lane synagogue which began life as a Huguenot chapel now became a mosque. The Bangladeshis arrived at a time of great racial tension, and violence in Brick Lane became commonplace in the 1970s and 80s. 1978 was a particularly vicious year. Like the West Indians who arrived earlier – after the Second World War – they have brought a richness to the life of the East End. We shall see whether they follow their Jewish predecessors and move out to leafier parts of London as they become wealthy. Some have already done so. If this happens the next immigrants may well be the City business people whose offices are now spilling over the City borders. The recession has meant a fifth of the offices in the Square Mile are unoccupied so even with the lower rents of Whitechapel the future of the area seems uncertain. Huge rail bills may well force middle-class families to be the next immigrants in Spitalfields and Aldgate.

Jack the Ripper

In Victorian England prostitution was part of everyday life in this area. It provided an alternate income to the sweat shop or service in sculleries and to many women it was the only way to earn money. At least they usually had the luxury of a bed for the night. Booth estimated that there were 60,000-80,000 prostitutes in the capital in the 1880s. The glamorous life was of course an illusion as pimps preyed on the girls, disease was rife, and it was a buyer's market because women and children were readily available. In hospitals the girls were often ignored or ill-treated and consumption and insanity would often follow syphilis. When in 1873 Samuel Barnett was offered the Living of St Jude, Whitechapel (which stood close to the present Toynbee Hall which Barnett founded) he and his wife Henrietta were appalled at the conditions in which the parishioners lived but they were also scandalised at the amount of prostitution in the area. They built up a number of clubs and organisations for girls with names like The Band of White and Good, The Guild of Hope and Pity and Mrs Barnett (later Dame Henrietta) as she had no children regarded the girls as her own daughters. She sold some jewellery to buy three local houses which had been brothels, used the rents to rehabilitate girls and even abducted an eleven year old child from a brothel to send her to friends in the country.

In 1888 Frederick Charrington the eccentric philanthropist and member of the brewing family led an onslaught on the many East End brothels. He brought private prosecutions and encouraged the police to raid known bordellos. Not all were grateful for his work. Bill Fishman quotes 'Misericordia' of Mile End who complained about 'religion armed with penal knuckledusters' and 'Explicit' who thought that one of the results of Charrington's work was to drive the evicted unfortunates out into the severe weather.

All these campaigns had little effect. Sailors on leave and wealthy West-enders demanded 'personal services' so the girls and their ponces remained in Whitechapel. The neighbourhood of St Botolph's was a place for pick-ups and in 1888 these became horrendous and vicious. The murderer known later as Jack the Ripper selected his victims from local prostitutes and the results shocked the nation. It is impossible to know how many women died at the Ripper's hands. The usual estimate is five or six between 6 August and 9 November 1888. All the murders were appalling and the wounds inflicted horrific in the extreme. The murderer knew how to cut up human bodies so could have been a butcher or surgeon. He was never discovered, which has added to the interest of the case and has meant he is now one of the East End's anti-heroes, bringing people to visit his haunts even today. He remains an enigma and Donald Rumbelow, the leading authority on the murders, once said in a talk at St Botolph's that on Judgment Day the Lord God will ask the real Jack the Ripper to stand up and a seedy, unknown man in the back row will get to his feet. Donald Rumbelow, always a popular speaker at the Thursday midday talks in St Botolph's, has written two books which I have used extensively to research this chapter – *The Houndsditch Murders* and *Jack the Ripper*. He is a police sergeant serving with the City of London police and a well known crime writer and TV personality.

All the murdered women were prostitues who plied their trade in local streets and in the small dimly-lit courts, cul de sacs and alleys. In the early hours of 7 August 1888 a policeman walking along Whitechapel Road was met at Gunthorpe Street by a man who had stumbled over a corpse in George Yard Buildings (which were at the rear of where Blooms Restaurant is now situated). It was a very shocking sight as the body was covered in innumerable stab wounds. The woman was identified as Martha Turner, aged 40, and the *East London Advertiser*, no stranger then as now to bloody scenes, was shocked that someone could be so brutally killed and no evidence be left behind of the killer. Three weeks later came more horror when half a mile away behind Whitechapel Station in Bucks Row (now Durward Street) 42 year old Polly Nichols was found with her throat cut from ear to ear, her abdomen ripped open so that her bowels protruded, and her body covered in cuts and bruises. Police Constable John Neil had also stumbled over the body as his beat which took only twelve minutes to cover led him past the corpse. It seemed the murderer was provoking the police because he slipped away minutes before the constable arrived. At the Post Mortem Dr Llewellyn thought the mutilations were caused by a left-handed person using a stout backed knife with a 6 inch blade such as a cork cutter or shoe maker might use. The victim's possessions were a comb, white handkerchief and a broken mirror and her petticoats were stencilled with the mark of the Lambeth Workhouse. This helped to identify her and it was found she had been sleeping in a lodging house in Thrawl Street for six weeks but that evening had been turned away as she did not possess the required fourpence for a bed.

A week later at 6 am on the 8 September the mutilitated body of Annie Chapman was found at the rear of 29 Hanbury Street in Spitalfields. Seventeen people slept in the house and the back yard was used by prostitutes for pick ups. Annie had been last seen at 5.30 am on her way to the morning market talking to a foreigner of about forty, taller than her. There was no evidence of a struggle but her throat had been so severely cut that her head was almost severed from her body. Annie had lived at 35 Dorset Street, a lodging house, for the past four months but on the previous evening despite being in the kitchen until 2 am she did not rent a bed. She explained to the owner she had been ill and so was penniless. Would he trust her for the rent money? He refused so she said she would go and earn the money and return. Her injuries were appalling. Her intestines had been removed and placed on her shoulder and two-thirds of the bladder had also been removed. It was the work of someone knowledgeable in surgery and anatomy, and would have taken at least fifteen minutes to perpetrate. The divisional surgeon, Dr Bagster Phillips, reckoned that if he had performed this sort of operation professionally it would take an hour.

The police began to receive letters signed 'Jack the Ripper' in which he told them what he would do. The Press reported events in great detail and panic hit East London. Samuel Montagu offered £100 reward for finding the murderer but no evidence was anywhere available. No one had seen a man covered in blood and anyway this was a common sight due to the large number of slaughter-houses in Aldgate. The only clue so far was the description of 'the foreigner'.

A double murder shocked the nation on 30 September. In the early hours of the morning in a darkened court off Berner Street, a turning off Commercial Street, a costermonger was returning with his barrow when the horse shied at what looked like a pile of rubbish. It was in fact the body of Elizabeth Stride and it was obvious that she had only just been killed. The nearby Working Men's Club still had lighted windows and the man with the barrow was the steward of the club, Louis Diem Schutz. He later said he thought the body lay in about two quarts of blood. The police searched everyone in the club and at the local houses for bloodstains on their clothing but nothing was found. Only 35 minutes later, at 1.35 am another body was found in the south west corner of Mitre Square (where the double gates of the Cass School playground now stand). The school had not yet been built so the two sides of the Square were warehouses belonging to Kearley & Tonge and empty houses stood on the other two sides. Every 15 minutes a City policeman patrolled by. As this was inside the Square Mile the City Police were now involved. The Assistant Commissioner, Henry Smith, had put nearly one third of his force into plain clothes hoping to catch The Ripper but in the event his constable missed the murder by fifteen minutes. Catherine Eddowes's throat had been cut and she too had been brutally mutilated. Part of the right ear had been cut off and her dress like the other victims was pushed up to her waist. Catherine had been in Bishopsgate Police Station earlier that evening having been found drunk on a pavement in Aldgate. At midnight she was heard singing in the cells and a half hour later she was released and walked towards St Botolph's. As with all the others her life had been a mixture of poverty, suffering and hardship. Having left her husband she lived in a lodging house with a man called John Kelly. Both drank heavily and summer hop-picking was their only break in a very hard life. At the mortuary it was discovered that a piece of her apron was missing. This was later found in Goulston Street covered in blood having been used to wipe the murder weapon. As Constable Alfred Long picked it up he saw scrawled in chalk on the wall, 'The Juwes are not the Men that will be Blamed for Nothing.' The police searched the area but no more clues were found and amazingly Superintendent Arnold of the Metropolitan police wanted the words rubbed out before a photograph could be taken. He said he feared an anti-Jewish riot. Sir Charles Warren, Metropolitan Police Commissioner, arrived at 5 am and ordered the words to be erased. Donald Rumbelow's *Complete Jack the Ripper* describes the events of that terrible night in great detail.

The *East London Advertiser* noted that Catherine had been murdered on the site of Holy Trinity Monastery. The writer said he had consulted an old manuscript which told of a monk who murdered a woman and laid her near the altar of the monastery. A curse was pronounced on the spot and having consulted old maps he discovered the altar stood on the site of Mitre Square.

The last victim was Mary Jean Kelly who on the 9 November was found in a filthy room in Millers Court off Dorset Street. Her body had been skillfully dismantled and her innards strung around the room. A wave of sympathy went towards this young woman, three months pregnant, who had no home or relations. A scream had been heard by two people but neither had taken any notice so once again the murderer escaped. Like the others, Kelly was trying to earn the money to pay her rent debt which was thirty-five shillings.

The murders now ended, the police had no suspects or clues. It was inevitable that people felt that no Englishman could do such dastardly deeds: it must be a foreigner. Other suggestions were put forward. Donald Rumbelow in his research discovered a letter from a woman in the Isle of Wight who thought a large ape belonging to a wild beast show was responsible and another letter suggested that male police shave their heads, dress as women and wear a metal corset and a flexible band of steel at the throat to catch the murderer. Just the outfit for an agent provocateur.

The police received several letters purporting to be from the Ripper and one enclosed a piece of kidney which was subjected to several tests at the London Hospital. The letter addressed 'From Hell' arrived on 16 October. At the post mortem on Catherine Eddowes it had been found that a kidney was missing and the doctors now felt this was it. Several other letters had also been received but it is impossible to know today whether they were from the Ripper. Who was he? Various suspects have been named including Montague Druitt, a 41 year old doctor who disappeared after the last murder and whose body was found floating in the Thames seven weeks later. Another is a Polish Jew, Kosminski, who lived in Whitechapel, had a hatred of women, especially prostitutes, and had strong homicidal tendencies. He was removed to an asylum about March 1889. Yet another is George Chapman, born Klosowski, in Poland, 1865.

He was a barber surgeon and was convicted for poisoning three women and hanged in 1903. All the Ripper murders were committed when Chapman was working in Whitechapel. Dr Neill Cream when he was being hanged in 1892 for poisoning four prostitutes said on the scaffold 'I am Jack the' just as the bolt was drawn. He was however, in jail at the time of the Ripper murders. The most famous suspect is a grandson of Queen Victoria, Eddy, Duke of Clarence, the eldest son of the Prince of Wales (later King Edward VII). Various allegations have been made but he was in Scotland at the time of one murder and taking part in his father's birthday celebrations at Sandringham on another murder night. Donald Rumbelow considers the suspects in great detail including William Stewart's idea that the killer was Jill the Ripper. No clear identification can be made says Rumbelow.

At the height of the horror Canon Barnett wrote to *The Times* positing practical suggestions – efficient police supervision, adequate lighting and cleaning of the dingy courts and alleys in his parish together with control of tenements by responsible landlords to stop under leases which cause so much suffering. The enormous publicity surrounding the murders did in fact lead to better gas lighting and even the proposal of electric lighting in Whitechapel. New housing policies were also implemented and *The Lancet* led a campaign for better public health legislation. 'It seems that modern society is more promptly awakened to a sense of duty by the knife of a murderer than by the pens of many earnest writers.'

The Houndsditch Murders

Amongst the great crowd of immigrants in East London at the turn of the century were political refugees from Tsarist Russia. I was reminded of these when we went into the attic of the Whitechapel Post Office fifteen years ago (St Botolph's has a flat on the top floor for a member of staff) we discovered a collection of Russian banknotes, share certificates and promisory notes. All worthless.

After the 1905 abortive uprising in Russia many activists fled to England to continue their propaganda war. In June 1907 a young man called Stalin shared a room in Whitechapel with Litvinov, the communist party organiser in Riga. Among the many groups of exiles were the largely anarchist 'Flame' group of young men and women from Latvia who were ready to kill and be killed to get money for their cause. In January 1909 an attempted wage snatch in North London led to what was later called the 'Tottenham Outrage' where two people had been killed and twenty one injured. The two thieves, Jacob and Hefield were killed but it was widely believed they were part of a larger anarchist gang. It was these who perpetrated the Houndsditch murders a year later. The British Government already knew of the existence of the Anarchist Groups and tolerated them providing they did not break the law or become too noisy. Extradition would be a lengthy legal business and probably unpopular as everyone was shocked at the barbaric, gruesome stories of Russian prisons.

William Sokoloff, one of the refugees, knew the City and suggested that a wealthy jewellers shop at 119 Houndsditch be raided. It stood where the London Guildhall University now has is administrative headquarters. Behind the shop and only separated by a tiny 4 ft yard were tiny dwellings known as Exchange Buildings reached by a cul-de-sac off Cutler Street. They rented Nos 9 and 11 then by good fortune No10 was left empty so on Friday 16 December 1910 four men and one woman entered the houses and began to break through the dividing wall at 7 pm. They hammered at the lavatory wall to get through to the shop and one of them Yourka Dubof, the locksmith, was sent out to see if anyone had heard them. As it was the eve of the Jewish Sabbath the streets were deserted. George Gardstein, Max Smoller and Jacob Peters continued their work. Peter the Painter was not there but waiting nearby at Whitechapel.

Next door to the jeweller's shop lived Max Weil, his wife and maid. He came home at 10 pm to discover the women anxious and upset at the noise next door. He walked to Bishopsgate and found constable Walter Piper. Together they went to No 11 and knocked. The door was opened furtively and their suspicions were roused. Piper said the first thing that came intoahis head 'Is the missis in?' Gardstein replied, 'She has gone out.' As he left, one of the thieves looked out and saw him call at No 12 to find out where the shop was in relation to the houses. Piper decided to go back to Bishopsgate Police Station and on the way alerted two constables Walter Choat and Ernest Woodhams to keep watch. Mr Weil told his story to the duty sergeant, Robert Bentley, who then accompanied him to the shop. Meanwhile the neighbour on the other side, Mrs Jones, who had a dairy shop was also talking to the police who had arrived.

The place being surrounded, Sgt Bentley followed by Sgt Bryant went behind the jeweller's shop into Exchange Buildings and knocked at No 11. Unfortunately the probationer constable Piper had not told him he had already been there. Gardstein opened the door and ignored the question, 'have you been working or knocking here? Fetch someone who can speak English.' Bentley waited as the door closed. Opposite at No 5 a young 16 year old girl, Bessie Jacobs, opened her door and saw the police in their heavy great coats and helmets. She recognised Constable Choat, a huge muscular man 6'4" tall whom she had not seen for a while.

The lights in the pub went out and the tiny road was darkened as one of the police shouted, 'Open the door or we are going to smash it in.' Sgt Bentley pushed open the door and stepped into the living rooms where a large fire burnt in the grate. He realised someone was standing on the stairs. Suddenly the back door was flung open and Peters carrying a pistol fired at Bentley as did Gardstein on the stairs. They had probably been warned by Dubof and assumed that the police would be armed. All of them had been ill-treated by the Russian police and expected to be shown no mercy. Bentley collapsed backwards over the doorstep and Gardstein fired again hitting Bryant in the arm and chest. He staggered back into the cul-de-sac and crawled away which probably saved his life. Constable Woodhams ran forward to help Bentley but was shot and fell unconscious. Sgt Tucker came forward and was shot in the hip and in the heart. He staggered the full length of the the cul-de-sac and collapsed, dying almost instantly. Nina Vasilleva came downstairs and ran out of the house with Gardstein. Constable Choat bravely grabbed Gardstein and pushed the gun downwards so the bullets hit him in his leg. Smoller and Dubof left the house firing their guns and Peters in an attempt to get Choat off Gardstein shot him in the spine. Choat fell and brought Gardstein down which meant he was hit by one of Smoller's bullets. Peters and Dubof half dragged half carried Gardstein towards Cutler Street then headed away from Houndsditch in to Harrow Alley. Behind came Nina and Smoller. At Borers Passage they ran into a tobacconist, Isaac Levy. Threatening him with a revolver they told him not to follow them.

Constable Choat despite terrible injuries from eight bullet wounds was still alive and was taken fully conscious to London Hospital. He was operated on immediately but died at 5.20 am. Bentley was taken to Bart's Hospital. Two bullets had partly severed his spinal cord. He regained consciousness and the next day was able to answer questions and see his wife who was pregnant. However in the evening his condition worsened and he died at 7.30 pm. Three police – Tucker, Bentley and Choat, died, two, Woodhams and Bryant were seriously wounded.

In all the confusion and darkness it was difficult to discover what had happened. 22 shots had been fired. Witnesses were taken to the Cutlers Arms pub on the corner and questioned. Sensational stories which did not agree with one another were told to the police and press. In the event it was not the star witness, Isaac Levy who was of most use. An anonymous informer went to the police a fortnight later and gave them the gang's whereabouts.

For half an hour Gardstein was dragged along by his two friends. Nina went for a doctor who refused to get involved. At last they took him to 59

Grove Street, a turning off Commercial Road to the west of Cannon Street Road. It was the home of another member of the group, Fritz Federoff, a locksmith. The gang laid him on a bed and fled. Later in the night a doctor did come but as Gardstein refused to go to hospital nothing could be done. Gardstein died early in the morning and the police arrived tipped off by the doctor. The link with the murders was easily made as the corpse had on it the key of No 9 Exchange Buildings and a pocket book of the Lettish Anarchist Communist Group.

The funeral of the three policemen was held in St Paul's on 23 December and the Lord Mayor attended in State accompanied by the Home Secretary, Mr Winston Churchill. On each coffin was the dead man's helmet. The Cathedral was packed and amongst the crowd was Nina Vasilleva already being followed by the police.

One New Years Day 1911 an anonymous informer went to the City Police and revealed the address of William Sokoloff who had planned the raid and Fritz Svaars another member of the gang in whose lodgings Gardstein had died. It was snowing hard when before dawn the police surrounded 100 Sidney Street, one of ten 4 storey houses built ten years earlier. Only unmarried police were used so they realised there would be danger and all were armed. The startled occupiers of the ground and first floors – twelve in all – were led to safety. Mrs Gershon who had let the room to Sokoloff and Svaars came down and was seized and carried next door.

Slowly it began to get light and the snow turned to slush. It was too dangerous for the police to go up the narrow stairs to the top floors so having cordoned off the road they tried to attract the men's attention. Eventually just after 7.30 am a hail of bullets came from the windows. Troops from the Tower, authorised by Churchill, arrived and a few minutes later Churchill himself arrived motivated by curiosity as well as duty. The famous photograph shows him top hatted between soldiers and police peering foolishly round a shop corner.

Nellie Ellis whose family have sold flowers in the East End since the turn of the century attended Sgt Rumbelow's talk and asked me why I had bothered to have a talk about the Siege of Sidney Street. 'I remember seeing Mr Churchill and the troops, it was all very exciting for an eleven year old but I can't see why you should bother to have a talk about it.' Nellie was amongst the enormous crowds who had collected and who were in some danger as the two men had Mausers with 1,000 yard range.

The police and Scots Guards climbed to the top of Mann & Crossman's brewery and surrounding houses and fired into the top floors of No 100. The wanted men came down to the lower floors and shots continued to be fired by all and sundry. One detective foolishly ran down the street and smashed the ground floor windows to the accompaniment of loud cheers from the crowd. The time ticked by and various plans to storm the houses were discussed and rejected. At 1 pm a shout went up 'The house is on fire.' Gradually the smoke became thicker then the roof collapsed and the police cautiously closed in. Two charred bodies were found which were later buried at Ilord Cemetery with no religious services. People were shocked that the anarchists were interred in the same cemetery as two of the murdered police.

Dubof, Peters and Nina Vasilleva were arrested after a two month search. Their trial opened at the old Bailey on 1 May 1911 and much to the horror of everyone the men were released due to lack of evidence. Smoller was never caught and Nina served only five weeks because the Court of Appeal said the trial judge had misdirected the jury. Peter the Painter, Peter Piaktow, is the man most associated with the murder but he was not at Exchange Buildings on 10 December. He probably helped plan the raid and shared lodgings with Svaars in Grove Street. His disappearance is a mystery.

5 FEATHERS OF BLOOD

Sir John Cass, his Foundation and Schools

Every February City workers are surprised to see the Lord Mayor and Lady Mayoress attended by the Sheriffs emerging from St Botolph's at noon carrying red feathers. Hundreds of children swirl around them with feathers in buttonholes or in their hair Red Indian style or being used as weapons for sword fights. It is Cass Founder's Day, commemorating the birth of Sir John on 20 February 1660. Baptised in St Botolph's eight days later, he was the son of Thomas and Martha who lived in Rosemary Lane (now Royal Mint Street). His death in 1718 was much more dramatic and spectacular. He was in his house at Hackney, sitting by the window, signing his Will when a fatal lung haemorrhage carried him away. He vomited blood over his quill pen, staining it red – hence the red feathers on Founder's Day.

Unfortunately he had only signed two of the Will's five sheets and a long legal battle ensued. He died childless and his earlier Will made little provision for the school he had founded. Lady Cass took the school under her wing and maintained it until she died in 1732. She tried unsuccessfully to get the House of Commons to approve the 1718 Will but on her death the Deputy of Portsoken Ward paid for the School's expenses until he died in 1738 when the school had to be closed. It took ten years to persuade the Lord Chancellor to prove the Will and thus establish a Foundation with 21 Trustees. Sir Crispe Gascoigne was the moving force behind this and his name appropriately appears on the Cass window in the Chapel of Peace.

Five years after Cass was born the Great Plague hit the City so his father, Thomas decided to move his family to a country village which only had 1,000 inhabitants. Thomas, a Master Carpenter of the Ordnance, settled the family into a house in Grove Street, Hackney. Land was cheap and he bought up several fields to make a good sized estate. He died in 1699 and was buried in the family vault at St Mary, Whitechapel. A portrait of him hangs in the School Board Room.

We know nothing of John Cass's education and upbringing in Hackney but on his father's death he became a very wealthy man and was invited to sit on the Hackney Vestry. He was 39 and by then a Colonel, married to Elizabeth. Despite being appointed one of the three Hackney Justices in 1714 he began to focus his interest on the City. On 23 January 1721 he became Alderman of the Ward of Portsoken but there was some opposition to him and it took three elections before the Court of Aldermen accepted him. After his death the Revd Peter Newcome of Hackney described him as 'A haughty, reserved man, neither loving nor beloved in the Parish.' He was popular enough however, to be elected MP for the City and to be knighted in 1713.

In 1689 a small school had been opened for children in the parish but there was still need for more so in 1709 Cass proposed a three-storey building should be erected at his expense adjacent to the church on the west side, next to Houndsditch. Shops on the ground floor and burial vaults in the basement would help pay for the education of fifty boys and forty girls. It must have been a squeeze to accommodate so many. There was a great charity school movement at this time and by 1710 there were 5,000 pupils attending such schools in London. The vaults proved a mixed blessing as workmen had to be sent to remedy the 'intolerable stench arising therefrom'.

The Archbishop of York, William Dawe, preached at the Opening Service of the School which was attended by 40 MPs and 16 Peers. Sir John's wealth increased and more land was purchased in Poplar but he decided not to proceed with his plans to open another school in Hackney. A Master and Mistress for the Aldgate School were chosen by Sir John who also directed that any child leaving the School to become an apprentice or to go to University should be given £20 per annum for seven years.

After all the upheavals following Cass's death the new Trustees, chaired by Sir Crispe, reopened the School in 1748. In winter children were to arrive at 8 am and in summer 7 am. They would receive a new uniform every Easter and commemorate their Founder by a day's holiday on 20 February when each would be given a two penny plum cake and half a pint of ale. The boys were taught writing, reading and arithmetic and the girls the preparation of accounts. A badge of tin bearing the Founder's crest was worn over the uniform and an idea of what this looked like can be had from the statues on the present Primary School's facade. The Trustees needed more rooms so asked Mr Kynaston, the Rector if they might erect a Hall for 'victualling' the children and for Ward Motes (elections) which were then held in the church. This was refused so the rooms above the Aldgate were rented for £16 per annum from the Lord Mayor's carver who had them as a perk. Here the children were victualled and the Master and Mistress resided.

In 1751 the famous sculptor Roubilliac attended the Trustees' meeting when they commissioned a statue for £100 and told him what Sir John had looked like. The statue now stands at the top of the stairs in the Primary

School and looks very grand indeed. Unfortunately the portrait of Sir John painted in 1754 was stolen whilst at the restorers in the 1970s. A copy from photographs was made but as it looked like a pub sign I consigned it to the School cellar.

In 1760 the proposal to pull down the old gate considerably perturbed the Trustees who asked for some land in Minories as compensation but this was refused by the City Fathers. Today the City Corporation own most of the land on which the present school stands and during my

Tim Mills

3   Statues on facade of Sir John Cass Primary School

incumbency I saw the annual rent move from £1,000 to £18,000 to £47,000. Negotiations are still proceeding to reduce this astronomical figure and perhaps sell the freehold to the Cass Foundation. In 1760 the Trustees, after the City's rejection of their plan, considered moving the School to Hackney but the Lord Chancellor would not agree to it. Instead the daily dinner was discontinued and the School moved to Church Row into a former pub. There it remained until July 1889 when it moved to Jewry Street where the London Guildhall University is now situated. Its final move to the present site came in 1909.

By 1818 the School had 90 pupils who were not admitted until they were 14. Four of the girls resided at the School House and acted at servants, the rest were mainly children of poor residents in the parish. Sundays must have been unbearable at they had to attend the lengthy morning and evening services at St Botolph's and after their free supper they were expected to recite the Creed and Lord's Prayer.

The Foundation's income greatly increased in the nineteenth century and several proposals to open other schools were discussed but defeated. The Charity Commissioners and the Trustees could not agree. The income was approximately £8,000 per annum in the 1890s and the Revd RH Hadden, Rector of St Botolph's, was greatly depressed by what he saw. 'There is no feature of administration which marks even the fitful recognition of a spirit of prescience or intelligence. Similar schools all over London adapted themselves to new ideas, to admitted requirements, to altered social circumstances, but Sir John Cass's School stood still. For nearly a century and a half it remained a monument of lost opportunities'. The self-appointed Trustees had power without responsibility and influence without knowledge. The Foundation weathered all the storms including the merging of Trusts into the City Parochial Foundation but in 1891 a bolt fell from the blue when the Charity Commissioners proposed reforms. They were resisted and delayed for four years and in 1895 the rejection of the Scheme was moved in Parliament but defeated. The proposal which caused so much trouble was the setting up of a Technical Institute in a building to be shared with the School in Jewry Street. In 1899 the foundation stone was laid by Mandell Creighton, Bishop of London, and it can be seen in the entrance to the present University building in Jewry Street.

Three years later the building was opened by Lord Avebury and the Cass Foundation offices are still situated in it. The Institute, now the London Guildhall University, has a peppercorn rent on the premises from the Foundation. In 1909 the School moved across the road and the Institute now possessed the whole building. Part-time courses were offered in science, technology, art and crafts and trade subjects, then a full-time day nautical school was opened which remained until a few years ago.

The Institute became the Sir John Cass College which merged in 1970 with the City of London College and King Edward VII Nautical College to form the City of London Polytechnic. In 1990 the London College of Furniture joined them then two years later when the distinction between Universities and Polytechnics was abolished, the Court of governors on which I sat for ten years adopted the new name of the London Guildhall University. Under the able leadership of Professor Roderick Floud, the Provost, it is now building on its excellent reputation in such fields as law, economics, banking and business studies, using its situation in the Square Mile to the very best advantage. The Cass link remains with the famous Sir John Cass Faculty of Arts, Design and Manufacture which has three departments, Furniture and Interiors; Communications and Music Technology; and Art, Design, Silversmithing and Jewellery. In the University for the academic year 1992/3 there were 6,761 full time students (47% women) and a further 6,500 part time students. Interesting courses are linked together as Nancy Hughes a third year student who in the current prospectus points out 'Although I took a foundation course specialising in Fine Art I decided that what I really wanted to do was study for a degree which combined design with business. The course at London Guildhall was the only one I could find which offered me this combination. We have a choice of two pathways, Design Management or Studio Practice'. The University has six teaching sites, four of which are close to St Botolph's – 31 Jewry Street, 100 Minories on Tower Hill, Calcutta House in Old Castle Street and Central House in Whitechapel High Street. The two administration buildings are at 117 Houndsditch and India House, 139 Minories. The students and staff add another exciting dimension to this already varied area.

The Schools

In the 1960s the Aldgate School was bursting at the seams. Archbishop George Appleton laid the Foundation stone of a new Cass Senior School in Stepney Way, close to St Dunstan's Church. In 1966 children from the former St Saviour's School and the Red Coat School joined the over elevens from the Cass School Aldgate creating the Sir John Cass's Foundation and Red Coat Church of England Secondary School. The first Headmaster was Geoffrey Barrell who was replaced as Head at Aldgate by David Jarvis. The Rector of St Botolph's remains an ex officio governor and I was Chair of Governors for ten years of Cass Red Coat and Chair of the primary school for all my incumbency. In 1974 there was a danger the Primary School would close as it only had 110 pupils but thanks to an energetic, new Head Mr Ted Broome-Skelton, the numbers have now climbed to around 210. On Ted's retirement in 1992 we appointed Mr Gerard Loughran who ably assisted by the clerk Peter Moss, now steers the school through the difficult waters of Local Management of Schools. The school has strong links with St Botolph's and benefitted greatly from the imaginative Wednesday Church Services arranged by Nerissa Jones. The religous education emphasises Christianity but includes teaching about all major world religions and as a large percentage of the children are Muslim it was a particular pleasure welcoming the Imam from the Whitechapel Mosque to take Assembly. During my incumbency a nursery class was established in the basement of the school and soon afterwards a Nursery Centre organised by the City Corporation Social Services Department. The Director, Elizabeth Crowther, and her staff made it a high priority to cooperate with the school in all matters and we were grateful for their enthusiasm. I chaired a committee made up of representatives of her department, the School, the City Education Department, Tower Hamlets and the Church, and today plans are laid for a fully integrated Nursery Centre. The children who come from so many different backgrounds are immensely friendly and I miss being greeted in Sainsbury's, 'Hello Wrecktar.'

The Cass Redcoat School, Stepney, under its able Head Miss Jean Hayes continues to flourish. Set in the middle of a deprived inner city area it obviously faces great challenges. 775 pupils are on the School roll and they are divided into four groups called Guilds, each presided over by a senior member of staff so that every child has someone to turn to in any difficulties. Depite the fact that the average stay in the school is only 8.5 terms (due to late entry or difficult family circumstances) and that a majority of students have English as a second language, the school's exam results continue to improve. Sadly the Cass Foundation decided to close its Rural Studies Centre in Machynlleth, Wales but has decided to fund school journeys to other centres. I visited Plas Einion several times and was always impressed by the care John Roberts, the Warden, took of the children in what was to them an alien environment. He told me that one of the first things the children did once they had changed into suitable clothing was jump into the stream and roll around in the mud. Several of them had not seen the sea before or been in the countryside. The atmosphere in the school is always friendly, robust and noisy and I often wonder if most of us realise what a tough job the teachers have.

The Foundation

Today the wealthy Sir John Cass's Foundation adminsters money left to it by Sir John and Lady Cass for their School. It gives grants to students under twenty five and to organisations in inner London whose work benefits young people's education. It owes much to Archdeacon Michael Hodgins, Chairman of the Governors 1963-84, whose financial expertise increased the Foundation's income. A tall, austere man, he had definite conservative opinions on most ecclesiastical matters. I once introduced him to an American friend, Fred Fenton, who waxed eloquent on the splendid work done by women priests on the other side of the Atlantic. The Archdeacon's frosty demeanour became even more glacial, and as we later said goodbye he remarked 'Take him out and burn him'. It was my impression that after his retirement the Board cared little for church projects despite the Instrument of Government's suggestion that they 'have regard for education in the principles of the Church of England' – only fifteen per cent of their income being spent on needy church schools in Southwark and London Dioceses. I thought governors meetings far too formal and cautious and those of the Bursaries Committee were often long and tedious as we listened to its chairman telling us at length what grants should be given. For me they were occasionally enlivened by amusing notes passed across the table by Norry McCurry, Rector of Stepney. Once he filled out a grant application for Mr R Whittington, 23, of Highgate who wanted to do a Business Studies course. The staff reported 'Mr Whittington presented himself well in feathered hat and knee length boots. We were somewhat surprised by the fact that he slapped his thighs continually and that he was accompanied at the interview by his cat. Another disturbing feature was that he suffers from delusions of grandeur and has, he says, church bells ringing in his head'.

I was always being told we had to be careful in grant giving but never once did we spend all the income available which each year always exceeded £1million. Sadly I also noticed that the governors wanted to distance themselves from their two schools and I was frequently told our grants to them were discretionary not mandatory. A recent influx of new governors including my successor and a very senior city banker might change the situation.

Sir John Cass's Foundation Treasures

1. The silver school mace used on Founder's Day and placed before the Chairman at Board meetings. This was offered in January 1758 to the Trustees by Mr

Robert Harley. The mace's head is a representation of the Lantern Tower of the medieval St Botolph's. The Minute Book says the staff had been used at Feasts of the Cockney Society held in the parish and may have been given to the Society by Sir John himself.

2. Sir John Cass's Snuff Box. In February 1755 at a Trustees' Meeting Mr Robert Bridgman gave this to the Foundation in a Shagreen case. Both were formerly the property of Sir John.

3. The Memorial Tablet in the Primary School Hall. In 1779 Mr Wyatt informed the Trustees that a Pewter Memorial Tablet 12" square had been discovered during repairs to the School. It says: 'In ye year of our Lord one thousand, seven hundred and ten and in ye ninth year of ye reign of our gracious soverayn Lady Queen Anne John Cass Esq born in this Ward of Portsoken did in his lifetime at his own cost and charge erect his Schoole and bountifully endowed the same fore ye education of ye poor children born in this Ward that they might be early instructed in ye knowledge of ye true religion according to ye principles and practice of the Church of England.

Ex dono John Silk'

4. Statue of Sir John by Roubilliac 1751. In Primary School.

5. Silver Gilt Loving Cup. Presented by Jeremy Bentham 1794. His father, Jeremiah had been Receiver (Treasurer) of the Foundation for 60 years. The cup is used to contain punch on Founder's Day. The governors drink from it pledging the memory of the 'pious founder.'

6. The 33 painted panels by Robert Robinson in the Board Room of the Primary School, which were removed from a house which stood between Botolph Lane and Lovat Lane in Billingsgate. The house, 32 Botolph Lane, is described in Mrs. J.H. Riddell's 1885 novel *Mitre Court.* The house was said to have been lived in by Sir Christopher Wren when he was building St Paul's. The hall occupied the depth of the house, 30ft. long x 20ft. wide. In one of the rooms there are paintings of Indians and 'two funny fellows riding on a rhinoceros and there are others gathering tobacco leaves, chariots drawn by some kind of deer, and sea monsters.' The house which had been owned by the Cass Foundation was demolished in 1906 and the panels together with a marble mantlepiece and fireplace with Delft tiles were incorporated into the new Cass School Board Room. The panels were discoloured and filthy from the fumes which came from the cellar in the original house which was used to store nuts and oranges. Before demolition the building was being used as the Billingsgate and

Tower Ward School. In 1904 the School was absorbed into the new Cass School.

The date above the fire-place is 1670 and was originally probably over the house's staircase. The panels contain the date 1694 and the name Robert Robinson who worked as a painter/engraver between 1688 and 1696. Little else is known about him although the Victoria & Albert Museum possesses some of his work which was sold at Sotheby's in 1954. Hugh Honour in 'Chinoiserie' says the School panels are the earliest known chinoiserie wall paintings. They combine themes taken from China and South America. It is obvious that Mr Robinson never left England so depended on travellers' tales to paint all his animals most of whom look distinctly odd. I particularly like the two small black men above the fireplace having a smoke. They liven up Board Meetings as do the large black ladies ordering the tiny white men around.

The panels may be seen by appointment. Contact the School Secretary.

6 THE CITY AND THE PARISH

The first mention of Londinium, 'a town of the highest repute and a busy emporium for trade and traders' occurs in the Annals of Tacitus after the Roman Conquest in AD 43. It covered 330 acres, half today's acreage, with 3.5 miles of wall which had six main gates. After the Romans left in 410 Ethelbert the Christian King of Kent built a church of St Paul in London and Mellitus became the first Bishop of the Diocese which covered Essex, Middlesex and parts of Hertfordshire. In 886 King Alfred recovered London from the Viking invaders and trade with Europe grew. The Charter granted by Henry I in 1132 recognised the county status of the City, and law courts were established. London's commercial growth continued and today in excess of sixty per cent of the world's foreign exchange transactions take place through the four hundred banks whose offices are in the Square Mile. With Tokyo and New York it is one of the world centres for foreign exchange, trading and financial services but significant changes are now taking place in the way market places operate. The major upheaval of the deregulation of the Stock Exchange – 'the Big Bang' – caused an influx of American and Japanese companies who were seen as predators and this has meant massive changes and job losses. The revolution in information technology has meant that the City has borne the brunt of firms changing over from people based systems to computer based systems, involving more job losses. The new Docklands and Canary Wharf developments present a challenge to the City Fathers but they have fought back furiously by developing millions of square feet of office space in the late 1980s, much of which is still empty.

The City Corporation is the oldest and smallest local Council in Britain with only about 5,000 people living within the City boundaries which were established in the twelfth century but shortly are to be extended slightly, particularly in Aldgate. The Corporation's powers extend well beyond the Square Mile for it owns 9,000 acres of London's green spaces including Hampstead Heath and Epping Forest. It looks after four of London's bridges, the Barbican Arts Centre, Heathrow's animal quarantine service, the markets of Spitalfields, Billingsgate, Smithfield and Leadenhall, the Museum of London, the Guildhall School of Music and Drama, the Greater London records office, a Magistrates' Court, three private schools and the City of London Cemetery in Wanstead – one of the finest and most beautiful I have ever seen.

It has its own Police Force. Its Education Committee has an interest in the City Literary Institute and London Guildhall University and organises the inner London Careers Service but strangely it has only one school to advise – the Cass Church of England Primary School. It was occasionally hinted to me as chairman of the school governors that the School would benefit greatly by losing its voluntary aided status and being controlled by the Corporation. Over my dead body.

The first Mayor of the City was Henry Fitz Ailwyn who took office in 1192 and remained mayor until his death in 1212. After that the Mayor was elected annually, a practice confirmed by King John's Charter of 9 May 1215. He became a Lord Mayor in 1414 and today is elected by Liverymen of the Guilds but in fact the Court of Aldermen decide well in advance who should be appointed. The sovereign has to approve and until 1993 the Lord Mayor automatically received a knighthood. Only once has a woman been elected Lord Mayor – Lady Mary Donaldson. Lord Mayors have little power as they only reign for 365 days but should the Sovereign wish to enter the City in state the Lord Mayor has to hurry to the boundary and proffer the City sword, point downwards, then precede her in what looks like Baron Hardup's pantomine coach to wherever she is going.

After taking over and moving into the Mansion House he follows a tradition begun in the fourteenth century and shows himself in a grand procession then a day or two later holds a banquet to honour his predecessor at which the Prime Minister, Archbishop of Canterbury and Lord Chancellor give speeches. I always enjoyed watching the judges arrive with their trains being carried by someone who looks as though she is a waitress from Lyons Corner House. During the meal the Judges are allowed to remove their wigs in case they dangle in the soup or beef. I also always enjoyed the Mansion House dinners particularly those given by the Lord Mayor for the Bishops all of whom appeared in their eighteenth century finery. At one of these I was seated opposite a bishop's wife then living in the West Country. Over the soup she asked if I was married and expressed surprise at my reply. At the fish she again seemed concerned, the meat course brought another comment. At the pudding I was feeling distinctly harrassed when once more she asked how a personable man like me had no wife. 'Because I'm gay' I said. There was no further conversation. These glittering occasions were always enhanced by the episcopal outfits and reminded me of Mrs Runcie's story of her visit to a couturier to buy evening gowns soon after her husband was made Archbishop of Canterbury. The camp young assistant had not recognised her so she said 'The trouble is, my husband wears purple watered silk.' Wide eyed he replied 'Ooh, how trendy.'

The arms of the city are the cross of St George with the sword of St Paul, its patron saint. The motto is Domine Dirige Nos, O Lord Guide us. Obviously the prayer has been answered for despite civil wars, dethronements, industrial revolution, bombings and several Government reforms its powers have been left intact and its income is still immense. Quite apart from rate income the Corporation has revenues from two private funds, City's Cash and the Bridge House Estates Fund, the combined annual income of which is around £47 million. Many large firms pay rent as well as rates because the City owns the freehold of large slices of the Square Mile, West End, Islington and Hackney. Because of this the Corporation pays for a host of services which affect the whole of London and lavishes hospitality on visiting Heads of State and other important people at no cost to the public purse.

Today the City is unique in retaining a business rate and also in still having the Aldermanic system of electing councillors for life who can reject new Aldermen elected by the wards if they disapprove of them. The electorate is around 19,000 strong, only a quarter of whom live in the Square Mile , the rest have a vote because they pay rates, though limited companies are disenfranchised.

Most of the residents live in the Aldersgate, Cripplegate and Portsoken wards who only elect 22 councillors out of 130. Many of the elections in the twenty five wards are uncontested but in our Ward of Portsoken the wardmote or election presided over by the Alderman, takes place in the Board Room of the Sir John Cass's Foundation. One of the councillors is then named Deputy to the Aldermen and ours is Mrs Iris Samuel whose husband was Deputy 1968–74. Known as Mrs Fixit for her ability to get things done she was made an MBE in 1991 for her care of the old people in Petticoat Square and her hard work in the successful Three Score Club. Perhaps one day she might be Dame Iris. Party political wranglings are avoided in the City as the Corporation is non political although most of us can guess how members vote at the General Election.

In Roman cities much respect and honour was given to the Temples of the various Gods but when Christianity became the official religion of the Empire in the fourth Century these cults were abandoned and churches took their place, often dedicated to the apostles but also to local saints such as Bride, Botolph, Dunstan, Giles, Edmund and Ethelburga. Canon John Halliburton in his pamphlet *Churches, Cities and Dedication* says 'That Christianity should have filled the gap with the cult of the saints and filled cities with altars and relics and churches dedicated to the whole company of heaven is not (as some theological purists might have us believe) a capitulation to paganism. Whatever we may think of the language with which the communion of saints is presented . . . the whole enterprise is basically an outward and visible sign that the divine indwells the temporal, that the Church belongs to the market place and that the Church Triumphant is actively concerned not simply for the Church Militant but for the whole temporal order . . . The City Churches are of vital importance as signs of the divine involvement whatever practically they may do'.

Today the Square Mile possesses a Cathedral and thirty nine church buildings, one of which, St Ethelburga, Bishopsgate has been recently destroyed by the IRA. Three other medieval buildings remain. St Bartholomew the Great, St Helen Bishopsgate and St Sepulchure Holborn. At the time of the Great Fire, 1666, there were 109 churches, 89 of which were destroyed. Not all were rebuilt but 79 were open in 1700. Fires and the Luftwaffe have destroyed several since then and 17, including some Wren churches, were demolished in the nineteenth century. In the 1920s a Commission suggested demolishing a further nineteen, one of which was St Botolph, Aldgate although the tower was to remain. Agreeing with today's Templeman Commission they only wanted four great parishes in the City boundaries, but no one took any notice of this nor of Sir Denys Buckley's 1971 Report which recommended seven team ministries, eight individual churches with special functions and nine churches to become pastorally redundant.

The only one of Buckley's suggestions to be acted upon was the setting up of a small committee called the City Churches Grants Committee which administers the money received from the City Parochial Charities. Today it consists of the Archdeacon of London, the Area Dean, the Lay Chairman of the Deanery Synod, the Secretary of the London Diocesan Fund and a representative of the Diocesan Finance Board. It now has £1.5 million to spend each year on the fabric and insurance of the City Churches. This is money given to the City parishes over the centuries which was collected together 100 years ago to form the City Parochial Fund. From the same monies a much larger sum is now given to parishes outside the City and a further large sum is given to good works in Greater London. Critics who want to cut down the present share received by the City Deanery should be asked how they will pay the huge maintenance and repair bills of the 38 historic churches.

Some 40 years ago certain churches were designated Guild Churches to serve particular needs but this experiment has failed although St Michael Paternoster Royal still cares for the spiritul needs of seamen. Some churches have been used as a base for a particular piece of work such as St StephenWalbrook where its Rector, Prebendary Chad Varah founded the Samaritans and still shows many of us what it means to be a priest, pastor and prophet. St Helen's Bishopsgate with its evangelical emphasis attracts hundreds of people to its Bible Studies and Services.

Only two parishes today have resident populations, our own and that of St Giles Cripplegate which cares for the Barbican and its surrounding area so most City churches minister to the needs of the 300,000 men and women who commute to the Square Mile each day. St Mary le Bow shows how this work can be done because its capable Rector, Victor Stock, visits the local offices and each week attracts a large midday congregation to hear his dialogues with interesting speakers. The famous city lunch hour is now no more as many people work flexitime, eating a hasty sandwich and thus there is no opportunity to visit a church building for worship, music or lectures.

The number of City clergy is decreasing rapidly and churches depend on retired or non stipendary ministers to say the Midday Service for a handful of people. Every one agrees that the future will not look like the past, and the Templeman Commission reporting in January 1994 suggests that two thirds of the buildings now find other uses and four large parishes be created. St Botoph's would lose its parochial Church Council and become part of a team with St Magnus the Martyr under the care of All Hallows by the Tower; St Helen's Bishopsgate would have St Margaret Lothbury; St Bartholomew the Great preside over St Brides, St Mary le Bow and St Laurence Jewry and St Giles Cripplegate over St Mary Woolnoth and St James Galickhythe. Discussions will now take place with all interested parties and my own somewhat biassed view is that the parishes should be increased to five with St Botolph's taking St Katharine Cree as offices and a centre for Urban Studies. Housing the clergy would be no problem as sixteen City clergy already live close to their churches.

The reserved churches which the Commission suggests find another use present an interesting challenge although All Hallows London Wall already hosts the Council for the Care of Churches, St Bartholomew the Less is a hospital chapel, St Nicholas Cole Abbey is Church of Scotland, St Martin Ludgate will assist St Pauls Cathedral as a travellers' centre, St Andrew Holborn houses Stepney Area Offices, St Vedast's is a Centre of Spiritual Direction and St Stephen Wallbrook hosts the Samaritans. This leaves eleven or so to find new uses.

Over the last twenty years the pattern of life is changing and it is getting increasingly difficult to build bridges with the business community. Following the example of All Hallows by the Tower I arranged weekly talks which attracted 20-50 people. The only exception was Donald Rumbelow's *Who was Jack the Ripper?* which filled the Church. I also established a Business Houses Council asking twelve of the larger local firms to send a representative to a bi-monthly committee held over lunch. The weekly talks changed to monthly talks and we drew large crowds to hear speakers who included HRH Princess Anne, Ted Heath, Merlin Rees, Jonathan Porritt and Vivien Stern. When Desmond Tutu came to speak the church upstairs and downstairs was full to capacity. After his first talk we had to push everyone out of the main door in order that school children could get in the side door to hear the Archbishop. Often a city person would chair proceedings and on this occasion it was my good friend John Ewington, a close friend of Desmond Tutu.

Not all meetings were so peaceful. When Sir Keith Joseph, Education Minister, spoke to a full Church I was the Chairman and became very distressed when a student seated in the front row refused to shop shouting slogans objecting to Government policies. Sir Keith remained seated whilst I told the student he must allow the Minister to speak. I asked three times then signalled to the police to eject the man which they did. I felt very embarrassed indeed not least because Sir Keith had been Alderman of our Ward, following in the steps of his father.

The Business Houses Council meant that St Botolph's had a friendly relationship with all the large firms in the area and could host their Carol services and Memorial services. When Eagle Star arrived in the building next to us I called on Tom Alder, a senior staff member, who soon became an enthusiastic supporter. In their first month I laid on 'Tea with the Vicar – including cucumber sandwiches' after their working day and over a third of their staff came to look round the church and crypt. All the firms supported the crypt work generously and this book has been paid for by them. One morning soon after Eagle Star's arrival I received a telephone call from someone whose office was on their eighth floor telling me a man was rolling up the lead on the church roof. I quickly phoned the police who persuaded the gentleman to come down. When asked what he was doing he told us he had climbed up there for a rest. 'Arrest is what I'm here for' said the copper who took him off to the station.

The Portsoken Ward Club

I always enjoyed the noisy, boisterous committee meetings of the Club. When they were held in the church tourists often looked shocked at the raised voices and loud disagreements but we never came to fisticuffs and usually we ended in peace and harmony. The Club was founded in 1924, in the Vestry Hall, Minories. Its aim is to bring together whose who live and work in the Ward, each year a series of social functions are held the highlight of which is the Civic Reception in Guildhall. During my year as

Master of the Club we held a Service in St Botoph's followed by a historical talk over supper in the school and later in the year we received warm hospitality from Bevis Marks Synagogue. The two treasures of the Club are a beautiful silver rose bowl given by Alderman Isidore Jacobs and a Master's Badge donated by Herbert Wolman. Membership today stands at 103. Recent Masters are:

1974	Walter Goldsmith	1984	Alfred Bush
1975	G Slater	1985	Deputy Iris Samuel
1976	George Pollock	1986	Herbert Wolman
1977	Councillor Arthur Brighton	1987	John Christian
1978	Frederick Ellis	1988	Councillor Alfred Dunitz
1979	Alex Ellis	1989	Councillor Roger Brighton
1980	Councillor Geoffrey Lawson	1990	Henry Packford
1981	Deputy Iris Samuel	1991	John Holt
1982	The Revd Malcolm Johnson	1992	Brian Bodycombe
1983	William Dove	1993	Evelyn Wortley

The first president was Alderman Isidore Jacobs. The president today is Alderman Sir Peter Levene.

The Congregation

Presiding at the Eucharist at St Botolph's was always a moving experience for me as I would look across the altar at the assortment of people assembled to worship the Lord their God in Jesus Christ. His Spirit had called together women and men from all sorts of backgrounds with different gifts and talents. The beloved Lois Wretham who is in her mid eighties and had worked for Norman Hartnell sits next to a young teacher and a landscape gardener. A multi millionaire finds the place in the service book for someone on income support, a woman professor of Computer Studies chats with someone who cannot read or write, Ronnie Moodly shares his experiences as counsellor of refugees with Adrian Parsons, benefit worker at the Mildmay Hospital, two unemployed people discuss redundancies and problems in the health service with Julia Reindorp, the church warden. Tailor and dress maker Joseph Akoto Mensa designs an outfit for Ivy Walker, a secretary from Sedgwicks who has taken early retirement to care for her elderly mother. Philip Weathers, a retired author and actor-manager teaches a young student how to read the lesson, Marybel Moore, teacher and social worker in East London welcomes a newly arrived member of the congregation. A married couple both in the police force compare notes with someone just out of prison.

Discussion groups after Sunday Services always go with a swing as no one feels shy in speaking amongst friends. No one turns a hair when one of the congregation always begins her remarks by saying 'I'm Hilda, I'm Alesbian, I'm Analcoholic.' A friend once complimented me on the fact the our community welcomed a transvestite every Sunday 'She looks stunninging in that yellow dress.' Unfortunately he had described the wrong person. Group discussion always revealed that the congregation comes from various religious backgrounds – Roman Catholic, Quaker, Spiritualist, Salvation Army and Anglican. All travellers on a spiritual jouney under the patronage of Botolph the travellers' Saint.

Philip Groom, lay reader, artist and former church warden, uses his many gifts to teach people meditation and also helps us to appreciate the Arts. He arranges exhibitions in the church and also invites outside organisations like the Wapping and Toynbee Groups to show their work on the twelve large display screens bought in memory of Father John Hunter. Perhaps the most colourful character of recent years was Monica Rejman whose home was in the local Salvation Army Hostel. Each Sunday she would be brought to church by Mary Waygood and caused a great stir by always wearing Polish national costume with its white lace cap, apron and multi coloured skirt with ribbons, and despite her zimmer she would lift her skirts, singing and dancing *Delilah*. Each year I arranged for her to spend a holiday in Southend with the Sisters of Mercy. Usually I took her by car but once I put her on the train and arranged for her to be met. During the late afternoon I received a telephone call from the Station Master at Liverpool Street saying she was sitting in a carriage on a train which had just returned from Southend. I rushed to the station and waved goodbye as rather like a parcel she started on her second journey. This time the Sisters were there to meet her. Another member, now dead, was over generous, giving me an expensive religious book most Sundays. At a meeting of clergy I sat next to the Vicar of the parish where he was a cleaner. 'It is a strange thing' said the priest 'but our bookstall seems to lose one expensive book each week.'

I always enjoyed taking communion to Gwenny Poulson, a forthright Yorkshire lady who Derek Harbord called 'My Favourite Battleaxe'. She was magnificently cared for by her daughter Sonia Poulson, a retired sister of the Royal London Hospital. The hymn books used every Sunday were given in memory of Gwenny who died in 1986.

The present congregation stand in a rich tradition of worship and service. I always enjoyed filling in City Business Questionnaires. When did your firm begin? Who is your employer? Answer – two thousand years, but this Branch 1,000 years. Employer – God.

Occasionally I felt apprehensive that such a small congregation, perhaps 50-70 on a Sunday, should have to be responsible for the large homeless project which existed in the crypt, beneath their feet. Fortunately we are surrounded by so many friends and supporters who sustain and care for us. Thank God for that!

7 A WALK AROUND THE CHURCH

On approaching the main door of the church we see to the right in the churchyard the sculpture *Sanctuary* created by Naomi Blake and given by her in August 1985 when it was dedicated by Rabbi Lionel Blue and me. Mrs Blake was interned in Auschwitz and says she seeks on every possible occasion to ensure the holocaust is not forgotten, so she dedicated the sculpture to all victims of oppression. On one of her visits to St Botolph's for Jewish-Christian events she noticed homeless people sitting with their backs to the wall and her sculpture depicts someone crouching against a pillar of faith, about to spring up refreshed. *Sanctuary* symbolises not a withdrawal from the world but a place where spiritual shelter enables faith to flower into practical action.

The outer glass doors proclaim 'A House of Prayer for All Nations' and the inner ones 'Pray for all who travel by land, air or water.' Abbot Botolph is seen praying on the top of the lantern tower of the medieval church. The design was also used for the silver top of one of the churchwarden's staves. The inscription above the inner door gives a brief history of the building – 'Third on the site from Saxon times this church was consecrated in 1744, restored in 1891, repeatedly saved from destruction between 1939 and 1945 and again restored in 1966 after damage by fire.' This reminds us that most of the memorials were moved, new windows installed, the font re-sited and the reredos covered with a curtain after the disastrous fire.

In the baptistry or narthex stands the white marble font which has an oak domed architectural cover carved and gilded like a miniature baptistry. Jeremy Bentham was baptized here in 1747. Above it in the ceiling is the large wooden trap door through which the bells are lowered and raised if they need repair. Above the ceiling is the room used as an office for twelve years by the Lesbian and Gay Christian Movement until amid much publicity they were ejected by the Bishop, Archdeacon and Chancellor in 1988. It is reached through a small glass door on which is etched details of the eight Aldgate bells. Next to the door is the signed photograph of Queen Elizabeth the Queen Mother who attended the Re-Dedication Service on 8 November 1966.

On the side walls are the names of the Aldermen of the Ward of Portsoken and the list of incumbents of the Parish since 1108. For some unknown reason Robert Peace Baker, incumbent 1848-60, is omitted.

The very fine Robert Dow memorial was originally in the gallery and depicts this Aldgate worthy in his best Tudor hat and ruff leaning on a skull. It was erected by the Merchant Taylors Company to their Master who gave many munificent gifts to various parishes and institutions including an exquisite silver gilt chalice dated 1594 to St Botolph's. The memorial says Mr Dow 'lived vertusly all his life tyme and dyed in ye true faith of our Lord Jesus', 2 May 1612, 'being full of daies at the age of 90 yeares'.

The Darcy monument is an exquisite piece of workmanship representing a sarcophagus on which is the recumbent figure of a naked man. Above is an architrave supported by delicate Corinthian columns and above again is a panel enclosing a coat of arms and crest. The inscription commemorates Thomas Lord Darcy who was a close friend of Henry VIII for 20 years and a Knight of the Garter. He absented himself rather than support the dissolution of the monasteries, and after supporting the rebellion called The Pilgrimage of Peace he was beheaded on Tower Hill aged eighty on 20 June 20 1538. Also commemorated are Nicholas Carew, Master of the King's Horse who was beheaded the same year for supporting Reginald Poole's rebellion. Other members of the family listed on the memorial were also buried here.

In the south west corner is the bust of Sir John Cass, born and baptised here, who founded the School and Foundation which bears his name. The bust is a copy of the original which is in the assembly hall of the Cass Primary School.

Passing through the glass doors and standing in the centre aisle we see ahead of us the modern design for the sanctuary with its theme 'The Gate of Heaven.' The three panels behind the altar depict St John the Divine's vision of the Holy City decribed in Revelation 21. Made by Thetis Blacker in a method of batik using dye and wax resist they were dedicated by the Bishop of London in 1982. As this is a gate church we imagine we are looking through the gate of Heaven to see the Holy City, the new Jerusalem, with its twelve foundations coloured according to the Scriptural account. In the foreground is the Tree of Life with its twelve fruits and from its roots the River of Life flows in all directions for everyone to drink. The angels in the side panels hold Alpha and Omega and guard the Gate.

The stoneware ceramic dove-pyx made by Juliet Pilkington holds the Blessed Sacrament. It hangs above the altar where Christ meets his followers in Communion. Heaven and earth meet. Barbara Sansoni's altar pall has been specially designed of fabric 'bricks' made of handwoven cotton cloth. The festal white side has a gold cross, the arms of which are

A MEMORIALL ERECTED BY THE RIGHT ~E~ WORP: THE COMPANY OF MARCHANTAILORS FOR
ROBERT DOW ESQ. CITIZEN & MARCHANTAILO~R~ OF LONDON & MASTER OF THE SAME
COMPANY & ONE OF THE CVSTOMERS IN THE PORT OF LONDON WHO GAVE IN HIS LIFE
TYME 352 ᴸ 8. 10ˢ. 8ᵈ. TO PERFORME. DIVERS CHARITABLE DEEDS FOR EVER TO DIVERS PIDIE
BRETHREN OF THE SAME COMPANY & OTHER VSES FOR THE SAID COMPANY, VIZ: TO CHRIST
HOSPITALL, TO Sᵗ. SEPVLCHRES PARISHE TO THE TWO COMPTERS, TO LVDGATE, AND
NEWGATE TO THE POORE. OF THIS PARISH TO Sᵗ. JOHN BAPTIST COLLEDGE IN OXEN
FORD, AND TO QVEENE ELIZABETHS HOSPITALL AT BRISTOLL.

⋅ 95 ᴸ. 10ˢ. 8ᵈ. TO ᵞᵉ COMPANY   320ᴸ. 00.00   TO CHRIST HOSPITALL,   050.00.00, TO Sᵗ SEPVLCHRES
100. 00. 00. TO Sᵗ JOHNS COLL IN OXON.   100ᴸ. 00. 00. TO THE CITY OF BRISTOLL.
HEE LIVED VERTVOVSLY ALL HIS LIFE TYME & DYED IN ᵞᵉ TRVE FAITH OF OVR LORD JESVS
THE SECOND DAY OF MAY ANᵒ. DM̄ 1612. BEING FVLL OF DAIES AT THE AGE OF 90 YEARES

...............ed by the Worᵖ: Company of Marchant. Taylors Anno: 1675. Mᵣ Robᵗ Mall̄ory

Tim Mills

4   Robert Dow Memorial, 1612

extended and entwined in the circle of the universe, with its symbols of earth, air, fire and water. The pall can be turned round so that the everyday side is mainly in shades of green symbolising the living and growing universe with the cross as the centre of all life. Barbara writes 'on the face of the frontal the dark brown earth entwines with the Spirit (white) to make two forms – a triangle for the Trinity and a circle for Creation which enclose the stem of the cross between them. I have made the Cross blue for serenity and peace and edged it with warm red for love and vitality. The two upright forms on each side of the Cross symbolise ferility and growth as do the many various shades of green; turquoise blue is for water and air.' In Lent and Advent the three panels and the altar are covered with purple cloth also designed by Barbara Sansoni and woven in Sri Lanka. The front of the pall with its symbols of the Passion and its seemingly unfinished edge represents the pain and horror of our world which is transformed by the Death and Resurrection of Jesus.

Angus Suttie who sadly died in 1993 created the two candlesticks and sanctuary lamp in exciting shapes and colours so that the eye travels up from the pall to the altar to the reredos to the pyx. All movement is upward as if pointing to the Resurrection.

Looking up to the ceiling we see the 1889 improvements made by J F Bentley, the architect of Westminster Cathedral, to Dance's building. The stucco of angels holding coats of arms add a new dimension to the worship. The shields surrounded by swags of laurel represent various individuals and institutions connected with St Botolph's. They are:

Altar:

West side:	East Side
City of London	Geoffrey Chaucer
Bishop of London	Lord Darcy
See of London	Sir Nicholas Carew
Abbey of St Clare	Lord Audley
Royal Foundation of	Thomas Howard, Duke of Norfolk
St Katharine	
Holy Trinity Priory	Martin Bond
Eastminster	Sir Humphry Weld, Lord Mayor
Thorney Abbey	Sir Hastings Stanley
Peterborough	Robert Dow
Ely	Francis Moriel
Westminster Abbey	Thomas Whiting
Edward the Confessor	Robert Taylor

John Clarke, Bishop of Bath and Wells	Sir John Cass
Ralf Joseline, Lord Mayor	Sir Samuel Starling

The stained glass of the church is made up mostly of coats of arms of the Aldermen of Portsoken Ward who have been Lord Mayor.

West side:	*East side:*
Sir Bernard Waley-Cohen 1960-61	Sir Frances Moon 1854-55
Samuel Joseph 1942-43	Sir Marcus Samuel 1902-03
James Shaw 1805-06	The Hon Thomas Hartley 1767-68
Sir Samuel Starling 1669-70	Sir Joseph Smyth 1684-85
Humphry Parsons 1730-31 and 1740-41	Sir Wm.Cuthbert 1748-49
Thomas Johnson 1840-41	

On either side of the central window are large windows bearing the arms of the archdioceses of Canterbury and York. In the Chapel of Peace there is a commemorative window to Crispe Gascoyne, First Treasurer of the Cass Foundation, Alderman of Vintry, Lord Mayor 1752-53.

The centre light of the window above the altar is based on Peter-Paul Rubens' painting of *Christ's descent from the Cross* and was given by Benjamin Standring in memory of his wife in 1857. The artist was Clutterbuck who also executed the east window of St Anne Limehouse. The original painting is in Antwerp Cathedral and a copy is in the Courtauld Institute. The glass surround is blue and purple which casts a dark effect on the window particularly as the tree outside also obscures the light. The glass was removed and cleaned in 1971 then in 1992 the IRA bomb in Leadenhall Street blew a large hole in the main window. The pressure waves from the explosion initially pushed the windows in but the following low pressure outside the building pulled the glass outwards. The damage would have been greater had the main doors of the church not been open.

During the Second World War a large bomb fragment came through the roof, missed the organ console by a few inches and went through the pedal board smashing it beyond repair. A secondhand pedal board was fitted and the organ patched up to make it playable for Services. Fortunately there was no other serious war damage.

At the back of the church is the bookstall which was given by SPCK and USPG to commemorate the visit of HM the Queen on 6 March 1980. On the wall opposite are memorials to:

Joseph James Redding 1856-1932
Frederic Pengelly Jenkins 1856-1906
John Sell Edmund Cotman 1848-1902

Cotman, a doctor in the Minories, was a relative of the famous Norfolk artist. He is described as a churchwarden, good, kind, wise and strong, a beloved physician.

Also here is the richly coloured tablet originally on the organ which says, 'This organ is ye gift of Mr Thomas Whiting to the hole parish, 1676'. Next to it is the memorial to Robert Taylor of Silverdale the Beer-Brewer of the parish who died aged 80 on 15 February 1577. On the other side of the door an alabaster tablet in a frame of scroll work bids us remember Sir Edmund Darcy who had fifteen children and died in 1612. Next to it a bachelor called Benjamin Pratt is described as a person of great piety who bequeathed the patronage of Greensted in Essex to the Bishop of London on the condition he offered it to the immediate reader or the most inferior minister of St Botolph's provided he be unmarried. He died in 1715.

On the western wall of the church there are two sketches made in 1887 by H W Brewer which give an idea of what this part of London looked liked in the reign of Henry VIII before the closure of Holy Trinity Priory which dominates the landscape. St Botolph's with its lantern tower and the water in the Hounds Ditch are clearly visible. Above it is the memorial to David and Mary Knox who died in 1833 and 1826 respectively.

Just inside the Chapel of Peace is the spendid marble tablet to the memory of Grace Barwell (died 1723), and her son John (1725), and William Barwell her husband (1756) and his second wife Elizabeth (1750). Also in the chapel is the new slate tablet designed by David Kindersley for the 250th anniversary of the death of Thomas Bray (1658-1730) which was unveiled by HM the Queen. Also in the chapel are the war memorial reminding us to pray for the 26 men of Aldgate who died in the first world war and the tablets to the Pouldon family and to Benjamin Standring who donated the window above the altar.

The Chapel of Peace designed by David Peace and Sally Scott was dedicated by Robert, Bishop of Lincoln on the 25th anniversary of his and my priesting in June 1988. David has etched in the screen the word peace in many different languages and Sally designed the Ark, the Burning Bush and the Descent of the Dove all symbolising God's presence with us. In a busy City church this is a quiet corner where the daily Services can be held and people can pray throughout the day.

The communion rails belong to the original 1744 church as does the tall pulpit with its baffling panels. Why should an Anglican church display a large almost Papal mitre in one panel and a Bleeding Heart in another? I can find no reason for this. Beside the pulpit is the sword rest for use when the Lord Mayor comes in State. It bears the Royal arms, City arms and those of the four City magnates. The last time this was used was when Lord and Lady Mais attended the service to rededicate the windows in 1973. For the Queen's visit in 1980 the Lord Mayor wore morning dress at her request. I was disappointed he was not accompanied by gentlemen in fur hats bearing sword and mace. It would have added colour to the proceedings.

The door to the sacristy is set in a new oak screen erected after the 1966 fire and the initials of Derek Harbord, rector, and Rodney Tatchell, architect, are incised into the wood together with their coats of arms. Inside the sacristy there are these memorials: a tablet in memory of James Matthew Roberton, vicar of St Botolph's and lecturer of St Olave, Jewry, born 20 December 1824, entered into rest 1 October 1885. This was brought from the Protestant cemetery in Milan where he died and was buried but subsequently his remains were brought back to Dorking cemetery in January 1886. A window depicting the Resurrection in memory of Mr Roberton was destroyed in the 1966 fire. A brass tablet in memory of Allen Winch, 1840-1903, 25 years head of Cass School. A plain tablet with inlaid marble border commemorating the Revd Michael Hallings, secretary of SPCK and for twenty years curate of St Botolph's. 'A true son of the Church of England, of great simplicity of manners and no less integrity of heart.' Died 7 April 1786 aged 50. A plaque for Mary Hallifax, died 1798 aged 80, and the Revd Benjamin Hallifax, died 1802 aged 37.

Outside the sacristy door but not in view is the brass plaque to Charles Glynes who died 28 December 1803 aged 46. He was vestry clerk for fifteen years and for most of the nineteenth century his family provided vestry clerks. Also commemorated are his son Charles Webster Glynes who did the job for 33 years, dying in 1836, and his grandson Randall who was in the post for sixty years, dying in 1896. Also outside, between the two sacristy doors, is the alabaster tablet paying 'tribute to the kindliness and worth of Arthur Hanworth Exham, curate of St Botolph's, who died on November 1st 1895 aged only 30.'

Walking back towards the main door of the church we pass a panel of seasoned oak carved in high relief depicting King David presumably playing one of his psalms on a harp. A pair of beautifully polished violins are among the other carved features of this early eighteenth century panel, restored in 1971, which came from the parish church of St Mary Matfelon

5   Eighteenth century woodcarving of King David

Whitechapel, which was destroyed by enemy action on 27 December 1940. Matfelon is the name of a herb which was apparently sold in the adjoining market to the church. Above it is a tablet to the memory of Mr John Evans, who died 23 July 23rd and his son John Harding who died in infancy. The next memorial is to William Hewson, and in the corner by the kitchen door a plaque to Jean Pratt whose remains were interred in the church in 1827, and her husband William who died three years later.

On the other side of the kitchen door, Alfred Lyon, treasurer and chairman of the Cass Foundation, who died 2 October 1904, is commemorated. Further along, above the cupboards, is the sad memorial to William Symington who died in penury and another to Robert Henry Hadden, vicar of the parish 1888-98 and chaplain to two Monarchs, 'a man zealous in good causes, steadfast in friendship, sober in religion.'

The crypt is not open to visitors but one memorial there is worth noting. On a Monday afternoon in 1985 when the floor was being dug up I was asked to view the coffins so asked someone to jump down and tell me whose vault it was. The breastplates on the coffins revealed it was the Vink Family vault. The very next morning I had a letter from Major Kenneth Vink of Carshalton asking if I knew where his family were buried. I telephoned and much shocked by the coincidence, he, his wife and his son came to Aldgate a few days later to see the vault. I asked him what had made him write to me at the very time we were exploring the vault and he said he had been reading the family history that afternoon and decided to ask if I knew where the early nineteenth century members of his family were buried. A plaque is now fixed in the crypt above the tombs particularly 28 July 1843 and Major Vink himself who died in 1986 and whose ashes are buried in the churchyard.

Three memorial tablets mentioned in earlier histories disappeared in the 1966 fire, namely those of Robert Silk, gunmaker, and his wife Martha, who died in 1699; Albert Oslift Rutson, a local teacher from Yorkshire; and the Revd Richard Peace Baker, minister here who is also left off the list of incumbents in the narthex. He died in Beyrout, Syria in 1860 having been 'compelled through failing health to seek the benefit of a milder climate'.

Before leaving the church why not kneel in the creakiest pews in Christendom and say a prayer for the staff and people of this place? May God be praised and people here be served for another thousand years.

The Church Treasures

The Organ

By a law enacted in Commonwealth times nearly all church organs were destroyed, but with the Restoration of Charles II in 1660 music and art regained their rightful place in church worship, so there was a great outburst in organ building. The two chief builders were Bernard Schmidt, 'Father Smith', and Renatus Harris. Shortly after Schmidt arrived from Germany and Harris from France, the Benchers of the Temple decided to acquire an organ and both were asked to erect one and find someone to play them. This 'Battle of the Organs' lasted nearly the whole of the year 1688 and Schmidt won. The plaque originally on the St Botolph's organ and now near the bookstall states, 'This organ was ye gift of Mr Thomas Whiting to the hole parish 1676' which makes our organ preceed the Temple organ by at least twelve years.

Mr Whiting was a man of some substance, a joiner living in Houndsditch who was Master of his Company 1677-8. In August 1676 the Parish Clerk recorded the burial of Frances Whiting, wife to Thomas and in the same year the churchwardens record, 'Pd spent upon ye organ maker when he moved ye organ back with Mr Whiting . . . five shillings'. It seems that Whiting may have presented the organ after his wife's death as a memorial to her. Later in the Burial Book the Parish Clerk records 'Nov 24th 1679 Mr Thomas Whiting Joyner of Houndsditch he gave us our organs.'

The maker of the organ is not mentioned in the Vestry minute books but several authorities have attributed it to Harris who also built the organs at the cathedrals of Salisbury, Gloucester, Bristol, Hereford, Winchester and Chichester (built 1678 and very similar to the specification of St Botolph's).

Originally the organ had a single manual and there was no pedal board. It is unlikely that the pedals were fitted to any British organ before the third decade of the eighteenth century. Dr Charles Padgham in his excellent booklet on the organ lists the present specification and takes an informed guess at the original specification.

During the rebuilding of the church the organ was stored in a nearby tavern and then John Byfield repaired it and installed it in its present position. Byfield was Renatus Harris's son in law and he succeeded as head of the firm after the death of Renatus (1724) and his son, John (1743). The present case was probably added at this time. The organ was later enlarged to three manuals and during the nineteenth century there was a rebuild by Messrs Hill and Son and in 1898 Messrs Bishops made further alterations. Fortunately it was then left alone and the old pipework remained.

6   The organ

In the mid 1960s the organ was rebuilt by Noel Mander whose famous Bethnal Green firm still care for it. The swell organ and its ugly box were discarded as were the nineteenth century additions. In 1980 the tuning of the organ was changed from equal temperament to Werckmeister III which is more suited to its period and character. Padgham reckons that it provides the best example in the country of how a Harris organ sounded in 1670 and that it probably contains more seventeenth century pipework virtually in its original state than any other organ in London. All who hear it testify to its thrilling, clear voice and for 25 years until 1993 the organist was Harold Dexter, professor at the Guildhall School of Music and formerly organist of Southwark Cathedral. His Mass setting and Te Deum were in regular use for Sunday worship, and I greatly enjoyed working with him. Another former organist was Dr Worgan who composed and first played upon this organ his hymn, 'Jesus Christ is Risen Today'. The present organist is John Bamford, who says he is looking for a rich benefactor to pay for a really good rebuild. Is this a pipe dream?

The Bells
In Medieval London most bellfounders were located in Aldgate, and Bell Lane nearby commemorates this. Richard de Wymbisshe cast a bell for Holy Trinity Priory in 1312 and in 1418 Robert Burford, a wealthy bellfounder, gave St Botolph's a bell and built a new steeple to house it. The bells were rung in the English fashion of 'rope and wheel' and the four bells were heard by Queen Mary I and her sister, later Queen Elizabeth I, on their arrival in the City on the evening of 3 August 1553, 'Item paid for the ringing of the Bells when the Queen came in, four pence.' A further eight pence was paid a few weeks later to herald the arrival of Philip of Spain. With the accession of Elizabeth came a gift from the Queen of a set of silken bell ropes because the ringing of the Aldgate bells had comforted her during her imprisonment in the Tower.

The sixteenth century parish registers record various happenings connected with the bells:

1586 Feb 9. 'We ded ringe at our parishe church for Joye that the Queene of Skotts, that eenneme to ower most noble Queens Majestie and ower contrie, was beheaded, for the which the Lorde God be praysed and I wold to God that all her conffederates weare knowne and cutt of by the lyke means.'

1589 July 30. 'The second bell being crackt was taken down and chandged with Robert Mott a bellfounder dwellinge in Whyt Chappell Parrishe.' The weight of the new bell was 9cwt 2qts.

1591 Sept 2. 'Robert Mott wedded Catheryne Doore widowe being of the Parish of St George in Southwarke.'

1591 Oct 20. 'The owld fyst bell called The Greate Bell, being cracked was taken downe ... to the house of Robert Mott to be chandged.'

The tradition of founding and ringing remained in the neighbourhood mostly because Richard Mott established the Whitechapel Bell Foundry in 1570 and it remains today at the corner of Fieldgate Street and Whitechapel Road. The bells were recast for the new church's consecration in 1744, the treble bell being inscribed,

> At proper times my voice I'll raise
> Unto my benefactor's praise.

The present bells are:

Treble	c 6.1.14	Thos Lester Fecit, 1744
2	c 7.0.0	T.Lester made me 1744
3	c 8.0.22 1744	T.Lester made me
4	c 10.1.0.	Thos Lester made me, a fourth to be 1744
5	c 13.1.4	Lester and Pack of London Fecit 1764
6	c13.2. 4	recast Mears London 1966
7	c 19.0.9	Lester and Pack of London, Fecit 1764
Tenor	c 25.0.7	Lester and Pack of London Fecit 1764 Henry Barlow, John Hirst, John Lee, Thomas Layton, Churchwardens.

Three of the 1744 set obviously cracked after twenty years so were replaced.

After ringing on Coronation Day, 12 May 1937, the bells were silent until they were restored and re-hung lower in the tower in 1966. Sir Bernard Waley-Cohen raised the necessary cash – nearly £4,000 – and once again the ancient bells were heard. Trevor Baily at the Whitechapel Bell Foundry carried out the work with special care as Mr Albert Hughes, the Senior Partner of the firm was Churchwarden. Derek Harbord had written to the Ancient Society of College Youths, one of the two important bell ringing organisations, saying he would only have the work done if they would undertake to ring the bells once a fortnight. When his letter was read to the Committee there was a long silence but fortunately Philip Corby of Sevenoaks agreed to organise it. His wife Lucille, his son and daughter and four friends came to Aldgate monthly and various visiting bands helped out with the other fortnight. When Philip and Lucille moved to Chiddingstone the Everest family joined the band and Philip Everest's son Robert brought his wife to live in Myrdle Street, Whitechapel.

For a short time Peter Rayner became Master of the Tower, then in 1989 Tim Mills and Keith Barber advertised for ringers in the 'Ringing World' and the new St Botolph's Aldgate Society of Bellringers began. They now ring regularly making the tower rock from side to side, but the architect assures us there is no cause for anxiety. So a long tradition of campanology continues. *Oranges and Lemons* has a verse:

> Old Father bald pate,
> ring the slow bells of Aldgate.

The bells have not always been appreciated by all parishioners. In December 1967 Mr R A Lewis who worked on the seventh floor of Portsoken House opposite the church wrote to the Rector pointing out that, 'for several minutes each day my work and that of others comes to a virtual standstill because of the ringing of your church bells. I cannot take notes while I am on the telephone because I have the index finger of my free hand plunged deeply into my free ear. It seems that people to whom I speak on the telephone can, especially when the windows are open, hear the bells but not my voice. Is it necessary, is it desirable for you to disrupt my work for five minutes in order to tell me that the day has reached middle age?' Mr Justice Harbord replied regretting that the Parish Church should cause inconvenience to business men but pointed out that, 1) the bells are rung electrically to avoid the clash and clanger of normal ringing, producing not much more than a tinkling which seems trivial compared to traffic noise, 2) the ringing lasts for only five minutes, 3) this is the first complaint received, and 4) 'one cannot help feeling that if property developers build offices opposite a tower which has housed bells for 500 years, they, (as we lawyers say), came to the nuisance.' Game set and match.

The Parish Registers

The parish registers and churchwardens account books, now kept at the Guildhall, are some of the most treasured possessions of St Botolph's, all of human life being recorded in them. We read of thefts, scandals, christenings, weddings, funerals, burials, (giving exact locations), and collections for worthy causes. Often the clerk could not resist commenting on the people concerned. Here are a few of the earliest entries.

1586 March 6th. A collection to relieve certain sick people in the parish including a fifteen year old boy, a 'ronnagate' whose toes 'were rotted off and it was thought he must lose one of his feet.'

1586 Oct. Baptism by Mr Heaze of 'Buttolph the Elder my goddaughter found in the High Street at the 3 nonnes gate.'

'Ellen Street, a child so named because it was found in the street the father and mother unkown.'

1587 July 9th. A collection for Mathewe Roe of Dunster, a ship owner 'who by the evation of pyratts and by greate losse at sea is utterlye impoverished and altogether unable to mayntayne himselfe, his wife and children. 3s 5d.'

1593 Nov 26th. 'The owld carpet cloth belonging to the Comunion Table in the church was taken away . . . abowt the ower of three of the clocke whyle that we were burying a corps. It was a Dorins carpet of the culler of sadd greene and popinjay greene,'

1599 Jan 27th. 'Averie Barwick a yoeman . . . who being hurt in the eye at Foyles in the Dukes Place at the schoole of fence . . . was buried neare the south end of the longe benche as we go towards the fonnt in the middle alley in the church.'

1601 Jan 31st. Baptism of 'Lancaster Stall, a bastard so named because it was laid uppon the stall of Miles Lancaster, a cooke in the High Street.'

1613 April. 'Hendrick Sturman, a Dutchman who dyed in the streete in ye night and in his drunkenness the 22nd day.'

1613 July 21st. 'Susanne Poynard servant to one Thomas Guest a glover in Rosemary Lane, who died by sore beating of hir dame . . . Thomas Guest and his wife were executed at Tyborne for the death of the said Susane the 9th day of August.'

1615 May 11th. 'Elizabeth Asher the reputed daughter of Thomas Asher, Houndsditch . . . who like a murderous strumpett cast her said child into a privie but by God's good grace it was heard to cry by the neighbours and saved and Christened, 10th May. Shee was taken afterwards and arranged but escaped death. The poor infant dyed within a fortnight after.'

1615 Sept 5th. 'Christopher Edwards of the Citte of Gloucester, Gentleman, and Martha Fosken of St Michael's Parish in Cornhill, widow, were married. The above were both lodged in Newgate the same weeke and he hanged shortly after.'

1615 Oct 17th. 'Thomas Addis, gunn-smith in the Minories who continued a heavie widower almost thee weekes, was married againe to Anne Basse a widow of Stepney. He was a heavie man at the death of his other wife but now is more lightlie geven and says, hang sorow.'

1615 Dec 6th. 'Dennis Green . . . christened. The mother like a filthy queane ran away and left her child.'

1617 Dec 26th. Baptism of 'Dousabella Portsoken so named because it was found at Goodman's gate in the Minories Street in our Ward of Portsoken, the wicked parents unknown.'

1619 Sept 1st. 'William Denis a porter and Joane Mellar Boeth of our parish were married by Banes. The Bride was a peece of crackt stuff'.

1620 June 12th. 'Erastus Hanson and Joane Holmes, a couple of lewd persons were married by compulsion. He an embrouderer.'

1620 Sept 29th. 'Edborow Allin daughter to Thomas Allin cooks labourer of White Beare Alley without Aldgate did open penance in our church, she was gotten with child by William Draper a porter being a married man who did private penance before the Minister, churchwardens and other parishioners the Sunday before in the vestrey house. A good whipping had bene better for them both'.

1622 July 29th. 'Edmund Dillow a porter and Elizabeth Lourey widow (a couple of old fools of our parish) were married by banes.'

1623 Feb 9th. 'Hugh Laurence a labourer and Dowsabella Morgan an old Rustie widow were married. A beggerlie match.'

1623 July 6th. 'Richard Dowde and Anne Hynde were married. The man was a bout 16 years of age and ye woman almost 13. By Banes a worthie ancient couple of young fooles.'

1624 June 28th. 'James Goodridtge of Oler, Yeoman and Marie Trumper were married by a licence. This was a fatt wedding.'

Today there is no clerk to make caustic comments on parochial affairs but careful records are still kept of the Banns of marriage, Baptisms, Weddings and Services held. Each January the staff are listed and this reached twenty two in January 1992. Numbers attending worship are carefully noted and it is interesting that nearly a tenth of all the year's worshippers are those at carol services in the fortnight before Christmas. I looked at attendances for Easter Day 1914 to find 35 came to the 8.30 am Holy Communion, 60 to Morning Prayer of whom 16 remained afterwards to receive the Sacrament and 56 were at 6.30 pm Evening Prayer. A children's service was held at 3 pm. Attendance on ordinary Sundays was about half that number. By 1920 the Easter attendances had dropped to 17 at 8.30 am and 13 at 11 am, and the numbers for Easter Day 1962 were 9 at 8 am, 27 at 10.30 am Holy Communion and 12 at Evening Prayer. Today the morning attendance varies between 45-70.

Parish magazines also give us a picture of past church life in Aldgate. 100 years ago in July 1894, the staff consisted of Mr Hadden the vicar who lived at 7 Devonshire Square, Bishopsgate, the curate Mr Exham, Mr Wood the Scripture reader and a parish nurse Miss Strange of 99 Minories. The sextoness (sic) was Mrs Burbidge who lived next door to Mr Cotts the verger of 3 Mint Pavement. The steeple keeper was Thomas Bernardin who lived at 103 Minories. There were three Sunday Services and Baptisms and Churchings at 4 pm if needed. Adult Sunday classes and Sunday School for children were held at 3 pm and a Mothers Meeting was on Thursdays 2.30 pm. Four schools are listed in the parish of which two held evening classes for adults.

The same magazine records that Tower Bridge had opened the previous month, three Baptisms and two weddings had been held, the choir had put on a concert and the Cass School had 202 pupils, (the same as today). We read that St Botolph's had acquired a vicarage for the first time since the Reformation and Mr Hadden moved into No 7 The Crescent, Minories in March 1885. It had been acquired from the City Corporation. Mr Hadden reckoned that the population of his parish was around 10,000 – at least ten times today's number. He had presented 21 candidates for Confirmation and he reports that the parish nurse, funded by the East London Nursing Society, had made 2,443 home visits in the previous twelve months.

Vestments and Hangings

Apart from three modern chasubles by Barbara Sansoni and a rather fetching floral cope bought in the sixties, St Botolph's now has no vestments of note. It was not always so because in medieval England the church probably benefited from the cast offs from local Religious houses. At the Reformation sermons were preached 'against candles, tapers, relics or images or kissing and licking the same, praying upon beads or such like superstitions.' Similarly vestments had to be sold and church records show that Robert Donkin, a tailor of Cornhill, bought a large quantity and presumably converted them into secular garments. Several pages of the churchwardens record book are filled with details of the vestments sold including 'three copes of red with lions and flowers sold to Humphrey Alton a tailor in Whitechapel, 41 shillings, together with copes of black velvet with flowers, crimson velvet, blue silk with beads, purple velvet with gold flowers, and embroidered altar cloths.' In the last year of the young King Edward's reign it was directed 'that all the lynen of the churches within the citie of London . . . saving that which shall be necessary for present usage . . . should be delivered forthwith to the use of the pore in the Spitall of Chryste Churche." After Catholic Mary's accession a cope was purchased for forty shillings. Pious churchmen added their gifts – Anthony Anthony gave 'a vestment of Blewe velvet and Nicholas Botrell gave the hanging that hangeth before our Ladie Awlter.'

The three reredos panels of the new 1744 church had the usual Creed, Ten Commandments and Lord's Prayer painted on them. The Victorians painted them over in the Burne Jones manner so that St Botolph and St Katharine stood near the cross in the centre panel and angels looked thoughtful in the side panels. These were badly burnt in the 1966 fire so Derek Harbord, wishing, as he put it, to create 'a drawing room effect' covered them with damask. He thought no reredos paintings were needed as the stained glass window 'fully suffices for interest and for piety.'

The Church Plate

St Botolph's has one of the finest collections of silver in the country, far superior to many Cathedrals including St Paul's. All of it is post Reformation with the possible exception of the stem of a 1559 chalice which might be medieval. The churchwardens of Aldgate realised that they might lose their plate if England became Protestant in Edward VI's reign so they sold a substantial amount of silver and presumably salted away the proceeds. As it was rumoured that City churches would only be allowed to keep one chalice, they sold two chalices weighing together 28 oz and bought a standing cup and cover (32½ oz) and a paten (5 oz). When the Catholic Queen Mary came to the throne the wardens had money in hand to buy more plate. Churchwardens, then as now, have to be cunning, crafty and thrifty.

The earliest surviving piece in the magnificent collection is an exquisite chalice marked 1559. There is no mention of its purchase so a devout Protestant probably donated it and inscribed it with the words from the Tyndale Bible, 'And he toke the cup and thanked and gave it to them saying drinke of it everi one for tis mi bloud of the New Testament that shall be shed for mani for the remission of sinnes.' It is the finest Elizabethan cup in the City and quite original in design.

Nothing further was given in Elizabeth's reign, but on 26th March 1606 Mr Robert Dow, whose memorial is in the baptistry, gave a very fine silver gilt chalice hall marked 1594, so it had spent twelve years in domestic service. The trumpet shaped bowl is engraved with foliage and strapping, the base is circular. Shortly afterwards another cup of secular origin marked 1609 arrived. It is nearly 14" high has a baluster stem with ornamental brackets and would originally have had a tall steeple cover.

The earliest flagon was the gift of Robert Hill, merchant taylor, whose widow presented a pair for it in 1622. In the first year of the reign of Charles I another domestic piece was donated. It is an exquisite tazza or low bowl in the centre of which is a classical bust that looks like the head of a Spanish soldier. The hallmark is 1589. The Goldsmiths Company have a similar piece which possesses a tall cover surmounted by a man bearing a staff and shield.

The chalice and paten (1635) showing scenes from the life of Abraham have a chequered history. When I purchased the cabinet containing bullet proof glass which still stands at the back of the church I displayed these two pieces in it together with two or three others. During a November night in 1983 someone broke into the church and using a scaffolding pole smashed the 'impregnable' glass cabinet stealing the chalice and patten. We were all fearfully upset and also angry because the alarm had not gone off. The engineer from the security firm who had serviced it the previous day had told me he had 'set the alarm' but this was later defined by the Company as getting ready rather than switching on. We were just about to take the security company to court when two days before Christmas I received through the post a scruffy shoebox containing the chalice and paten. My comment 'God bless the burglars' was widely reported in the press. The two pieces are important because the engraving of Abraham about to sacrifice Isaac was frequently used in medieval art to parallel the death of Our Lord and it would appear that these items are the only example of the use of an Old Testament subject on a post-Reformation piece of English church plate.

Not surprisingly there were no additions to the collection during the Commonwealth period but benefactions resumed after the Restoration. A huge 13" flagon weighing 71 oz , 'The Gift of MM' (Mary Masters) arrived in 1665 inscribed 'For Ye Sole Youse Of Ye Sacrament' reminding the congregation not to use it for refreshments at vestry meetings. A long handled spoon to remove flies etc from the chalice had arrived ten years earlier. In 1669 a flagon was given by Mrs Ann Sole. A rather sad looking

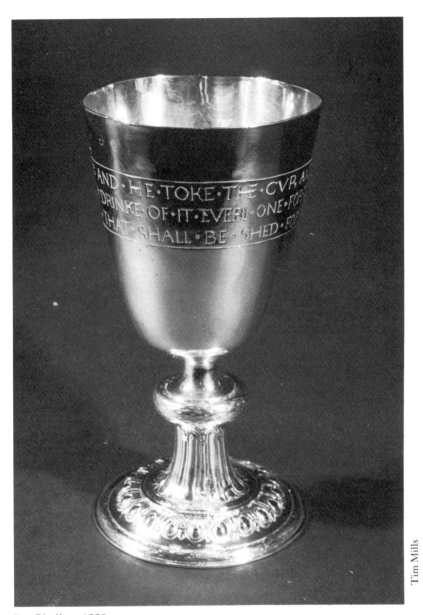

AND · HE · TOKE · THE · CVR A
DRINKE · OF · IT · EVERI · ONE · FO
THAT · SHALL · BE · SHED · FO

Tim Mills

7   Chalice, 1559

salver was donated in 1704 presumably to be used as a paten. Two silver tops which are put on the churchwardens staves are of interest. The earliest dating from 1748 is square and surmounted by a swan. There is an engraving on one side of the White Tower in the Tower of London. The other top is modern, made in 1930, and depicts St Botolph kneeling, surrounded by the top of the lantern tower of the medieval church. A pear shaped head for a Beadle's staff is inscribed with the names of various Victorian worthies. All three are still used regularly.

In 1974 I received from Sydney, Australia, a silver salver and chalice which had been in the possession of Mr Arthur Homewood who had been baptised in St Botolph's on 17 August 1896. They had been designed by his brother Walter and were sent to St Botolph's after his death by his sister Beatrice who lived in Croydon.

The Holy Trinity Minories silver, whilst not so outstandingly fine as St Botolph's, has some interesting pieces, notably a tall heavy pair of flagons given in 1669 by Col Sir William Legge who had been a fervent supporter of Charles I in the Civil War and Governor of Oxford. In 1649 after the King's execution he was imprisoned in Exeter Castle, then The Tower. At the Restoration he was appointed Lieutenant-General of the Ordnance and offered an earldom which he declined. His son was created Lord Dartmouth in 1682 and the family tomb was in Holy Trinity, Minories.

Also important is a silver baptismal ewer given by Philip Vaffree in 1683, and two matching pair of alms dishes given in 1730 and 1808.

The Parochial Church Council have had several discussions about the morality of possessing such a huge hoard of antique silver which must be worth a considerable sum. They have always come to the conclusion that the various pieces were lovingly given so should not be sold unless money cannot be found from other sources for whatever project is planned. If a decision to sell were made the Chancellor of the Diocese would have to give permission and a good case would have to be argued in his court. Sadly the collection is rarely seen as it is stored in a local bank strong room. The Victoria and Albert Museum once took some on a long loan and the Treasury of St Paul's Cathedral might perhaps consider showing some of the rarer pieces.

Inventory of the Church Plate

St Botolph Aldgate

1559 London. Silver cup, part gilt. Inscribed with text from the Tyndale Bible and engraved with the weight '31 oz and hafe'. Height 8½". Marks worn – probably a bird.

1589 London. Silver gilt Tazza with classical bust in centre engraved with foliage and strapwork, chased stem and base. Insc. SBAIRIG 1625. Maker, Edward Delves.

1594 London. Silver gilt chalice, V shaped body, balister stem and round base. Insc. 'This is the gift of Mr Robert Dow, Merchant Taylor, 29th March 1606.' 14 oz 15 DWT. 14" high. Maker's mark, TH.

1609 London. Silver gilt cup, decorated in the contemporary style with embossed and chased strapwork and Arabesques. Bracketed stem and round base. Insc. with weight 23 oz. 13¼" high. Maker, SF in a shaped shield.

1635 London. Silver chalice and paten. Engraved with scenes of the life of Abraham, the weight, and, 'Videt Deus Et Providebit Sibi Victiman Sba Ex Dono Tho: Soll.' Weight 30 oz (chalice) and 9 oz (paten). Height 7¼" (chalice). Maker, Walter Shute.

1665 London. Long handled spoon. Insc. S. Buttales Algeate 1665. 9½" long. Maker, Stephen Venables.

1669 London. Flagon, engraved 'The gift of Mrs Anne Sole, widow of ye Parish of Botolph, Aldgate, 1669.' Weight 34 oz. 14 DWT. Height 9". Maker's mark TK with a fleur de lys below.

1675 London. Silver Master Flagon. Insc. 'The Gift of M.M. To Ye Parish Church Of St Botolph Aldgate For Ye Sole Youse Of Ye Sacrament." Weight 71 oz. Height 13". Maker 'PP' set in a heart.

1704 London. Salver / paten with rope borders. Weight 12½ oz. Insc. 'St Botolph Aldgate'. Maker, Robert Peake.

1746 London. Dessert Spoon. Old English pattern. Weight 17 DWT.

1748 London. Silver top for churchwarden's staff. Square to represent the White Tower (of London) of which there is an engraving on one side. On the other sides appear names of the foremen and constables of the Manor of East Smithfield.

1861 London. Silver top for a Beadle's staff. Pear shaped. Insc. with the names of the foremen and constables of the Court Leet of the Manor of East Smithfield.

1930. Silver top for churchwardens staff. Model of medieval church tower with kneeling St Botolph.

c.1930. Australian silver chalice and salver. Designed by Walter Homewood. Maker unknown.

In use:
Two large modern silver chalices.
One paten.
One small silver chalice and paten.
One ciborium.

A large modern silver altar dish listed in August 1958 worth £25 and seen in various photographs has disappeared. Neither George Appleton nor Derek Harbord could throw any light on this mystery.

St Botolph's also possesses some fine large pewter plates which bear the arms of Charles I, so presumably were made in the second quarter of the seventeenth century.

Holy Trinity Minories

1637 London. Silver chalice with beaker shaped bowl and trumpet foot, engraved with a coat of arms. Maker, GD placed in a heart.

1669 London. Pair of flagons. Insc. 'The Gift of Colonel William Legge of his Majesty's bedchamber 25 December 1669.' Weight 44 oz 3DWT and 45oz 5DWT, both 7.75" high. Maker WM crowned.

1683 London. Silver Baptismal Ewer Insc. 'The Gift of Phillip Vaffree to Ye Parish Church of Trinity Minories, Arthur Roland Churchwarden 20 May 1683.' Weight 17oz 5DWT Height 7.75" Maker EV Crowned

1719 London. Standing paten. Maker Thomas Mason

1730 London. Pair of Alms dishes. $9\frac{5}{8}$" diam. Weight 30 oz Maker, Thomas Farrer.

1808 London. Pair of Alms Dishes. Parcel gilt centre, engraved 'Glory, The Gift Of John Judson'. Weight 30 oz. $9\frac{5}{8}$" diam. Makers, Peter and William Bateman.

8 A WALK AROUND ALDGATE

L eaving the church gate we cross the road to the pedestrian island which is the site of the Ald Gate demolished in 1760 for the widening of the road. It was one of the four original and most important entrances to the City, and was rebuilt on two or three occasions from Roman times onward. Its task was to keep marauders out of the City but it was not always successful because in the time of King John the Barons opposed to him pushed their way through the gate and ravaged many of the houses. The gate with its two portcullises must have been a magnificent sight.

In 1374 Chaucer lived in the apartments over the gate and in 1471 the rebellion of Falconbridge was put down by Robert Bassett the Alderman of Aldgate Ward which incidentally lies immediately to the west of St Botolph's. It contains our school and I got into hot water for not inviting the then Alderman to the reception held there for the Queen in 1980. I assumed, wrongly, the school stood in Portsoken Ward like the Church.

In 1606 the gate was rebuilt and many Roman coins were found in its Foundations. There were two posterns or passages for foot passengers, that on the South side built in 1663.

Crossing the road to the school we walk along beside the new railings and look down on the under fives of the Nursery Department enjoying themselves in the playground. It seems odd hearing children's voices in the City and John Carpenter of Guardian Royal Exchange whose office is on the south side of the road once surprised a Japanese customer on the telephone by telling him he was looking at children chasing a pet rabbit which had escaped outside his office. Along this south side of the road now stands a large modern building, but in 1862 the four storey buildings were, (from Jewry Street to Fenchurch Street) a fancy dealer, a ham and beef shop, Nash and Son Woollen Merchants, Barham and Marriage, Grocers; a restaurant, a hatter, Wiggins Teape and Co at No 7; a stationer, a fishmonger, Ashby and Horner the builders, a tobacconist, Saracens Head Yard and a confectioner. All but two were demolished at the turn of the century and none remain today although Wiggins Teape and Co are still in business as paper merchants. The firm's origins are obscure but it took up residence at 10 Aldgate in 1761. It was probably the first firm in the paper trade to send a commercial traveller out of London and the horses were stabled in the Saracens Head Yard. The name of the pub probably refers to the Crusades and the coaching inn of that name is mentioned on

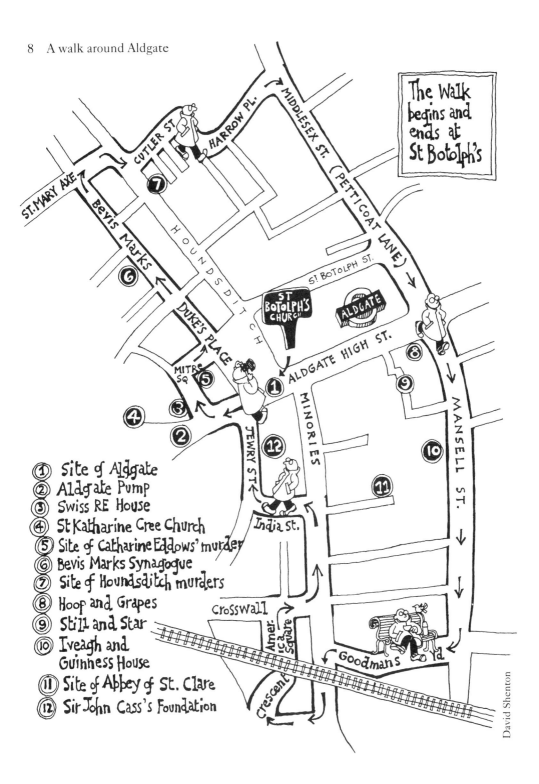

The Walk begins and ends at St Botolph's

① Site of Aldgate
② Aldgate Pump
③ Swiss RE House
④ St Katharine Cree Church
⑤ Site of Catharine Eddows' murder
⑥ Bevis Marks Synagogue
⑦ Site of Houndsditch murders
⑧ Hoop and Grapes
⑨ Still and Star
⑩ Iveagh and Guinness House
⑪ Site of Abbey of St. Clare
⑫ Sir John Cass's Foundation

David Shenton

a map of 1677.

Messrs Ashby and Horner, Builders and Contractors, are also still in business having been established over 240 years ago. The firm was in the hands of John Search until his death in 1784 when he left it to his apprentice James Bridger who became wealthy and was elected Master of the Drapers Company.

Looking ahead we see Leadenhall and Fenchurch Streets merging at Aldgate Pump. This is the spot where traditionally the East End begins. In early times it was called St Michael's Well and was described as the only spring water in the City. 150 years ago the Pump was moved several feet westwards when the roads were widened.

Stow, the London chronicler, lived in a house at the corner of Leadenhall Street, and slightly to the north of the Pump stood St Michael's Chapel. Several prints can be found today in antique shops of the subterranean cellars and crypt of this church which had painted medieval arches. The chapel of St Michael escaped demolition at the Reformation.

This corner has always been an important place – executions were held here in the sixteenth century, travellers have always arrived here by horse or coach from East Anglia, and in the mid nineteenth century it was known as 'The Five Lamps' because when gas replaced oil for street lighting there was a blaze of light around the pump.

Passing along Leadenhall Street we arrive at St Katharine Cree, one of the four City churches which escaped the great fire. Rebuilt in 1628 by Inigo Jones it was consecrated by Archbishop Laud. The tower is earlier, probably around 1504. Cree Church means Christ Church and refers to Holy Trinity Priory. The interior is disappointing as the north and south aisles have been clumsily converted into offices. The font is octagonal, marble, 1630 and the reredos was brought from St James, Dukes Place in 1874. The pulpit is elegant early eighteenth century and the organ by Father Schmidt, 1686 with a beautifully carved case. The east window of 1630 is particularly beautiful and the two monuments of Sir Nicholas Throckmorton 1571 and Samuel Thorp 1794 should not be missed. The church posseses very fine communion plate which was probably used by Laud at the consecration. Pennant, an enemy of Laud, has left an unkind account of the Service: 'When the bishop approached near the communion table he bowed with his nose very near the ground some six or seven times then he came to the corners of the table and there bowed himself three times at each but when he came to the side of the table where the bread and wine was he bowed seven times and then after the reading many praiers by himself and two of his chaplins . . . he came near the bread which was laid in a napkin, lifted it up like a boy that peeped into a birds nest . . .

then bowed very low three times towards the table . . . after these and many more apish anticke gestures he himself received.'

Each year the 'Lion Sermon' is preached in the church to commemorate the escape of Sir John Gayer, a City merchant and Lord Mayor who died in 1649 from being eaten by a lion when he was separated from his party during a visit to Arabia on business.

Walking back towards Aldgate we turn left into Mitre Street and look through the windows of Swiss RE house on our left to see the remaining arch of the great Trinity priory. To our right is Sir John Cass's Primary School built in the solid dependable style of the turn of the century. On its Mitre Street frontage once stood the Aldgate Ward Schools which were merged with the Cass school and also a large Victorian building, Essex House, which was bought in the 1970s to be demolished so the school playground could be extended.

In the playground of the Cass school once stood St James Church whose reredos we saw in St Katharine Cree. St James was consecrated in 1622 and possessed very little of historical interest. Its tower slightly resembled St Katharine's and was built by the City Corporation at the request of local parishioners. It was pulled down in 1874.

The large double gates to the playground in Mitre Square are very close to the place where the unfortunate Catherine Eddowes was murdered by Jack the Ripper on 30th September 1888.

Close by once stood the Great Synagogue, in Dukes Place first established as a small meeting house for prayer by the German Jews around the 1690s in Broad Court, Mitre Square but which moved a few yards in 1722 to a large building in St James Place erected at the expense of Moses of Breslau a wealthy merchant. Subsequently a more handsome building was erected by the gifts of many German Jews including £4,000 from Mrs Judith Levy, daughter of Moses of Breslau. It soon became the centre of much good work amongst the Jews of East London. A schismatic offshoot founded the 'New Synagogue' in Great St Helens in 1838.

Walking past the school on the right we come to St James Place, now a one way street south to north, and we turn left. We cross over Heneage Lane and come on our left to the elegant arch, rebuilt a few years ago, which leads to the Bevis Marks Synagogue. St Botolph's has always valued its links with Bevis Marks and on the Day of Atonement each year a party of thirty or so join in the morning worship at the Synagogue. Despite being badly damaged by the 1993 IRA bomb the building has a most wonderful atmosphere of prayer and the liturgy in Hebrew chanted beneath the large chandeliers is very meaningful indeed. The rabbi always welcomes our party and Alfred de Mesquita and Donald Silk make us feel at home by finding the place in the Service Books.

The Spanish and Portuguese congregation in London dates from 1656 when, having been permitted to resettle in England, the first Jewish residents are believed to have worshipped quietly in Cree Church Lane. In 1664 they acquired a meeting house in King Street, Aldgate which the congregation rapidly outgrew so a plot of land was purchased in Plough Yard, Bevis Marks. The new building cost £2.750 and it is said that Queen Anne sent a huge piece of wood from one of her old ships which was used as a rafter. Some of the benches (chavetas), were brought from King Street

9   Aldgate Pump

and brass chandeliers were imported from Holland. In 1701 the building was opened and in 1951 Prince Philip attended a special service to commemorate the two hundred and fiftieth anniversary.

In 1405 the City of London Records mention Bewesmerkes, and by 1513 this had become Beve Smarkes and in subsequent manuscripts Buries Markes. It is possible that these names refer to the house and gardens of the Abbots of Bury St Edmunds in Suffolk. Bevis could be corrupt for Beris the genetive of Bury. In some medieval handwriting R and V are very similar. Marks is the plural of a mark or post denoting a boundary, so the name could denote the boundary or mark of the Bury Land. After the dissolution of Holy Trinity Priory the land was given to Sir Thomas Heneage, Keeper of the Tower Records, Paymaster of the Forces and Vice Chamberlain to Queen Elizabeth I, hence 'Heneage' Lane nearby. Bury Street also reminds us of the link with Suffolk. Dickens spent a morning wandering round here to find a suitable house to describe as the 'Little Habitation' of Sampson Brass the lawyer in *The Old Curiosity Shop*. It was 'so close upon the footway that the passenger who rakes the wall brushes the dim glass with his coat sleeve – much to its improvement for it is very dirty.'

The parish boundary now turns right from Bevis Marks into St Mary Axe, which also had Dickensian connections as Fascination Fledgeby's money lending business, Pubsey and Co in *Our Mutual Friend* was here. The name of the street is taken from the church which stood here until 1565 and was said to possess an axe used by Attila the Hun to execute 11,000 virgins.

Turning right into Houndsditch we then immediately turn left into Cutler street. The jeweller's shop which featured in the Houndsditch murders, stood on the site of the present London Guildhall University Building. Its back door was on Exchange Buildings where the police were shot.

Cutler Street is thus named because the Cutlers Company owned the land. The huge warehouses in it were built in the late 18th century by the East India Company to house their goods, mainly tea. The Port of London Authority bought them and today they have been converted into a number of uses – shops, offices.

Clothier Street reminds us of the old clothes market that was regularly held here. In 1870 Daniel Kirwan wrote of 'hundreds and hundreds of pairs of trousers . . . fustian jackets, some greasy some unsoiled . . . drawers and stockings, the latter washed and hung up in all their appealing innocence.' Hundreds of people visited the market.

White Kennett Street is the only local street named after an incumbent

Tim Mills

10   Bevis Marks Synagogue

of St Botolph's (1700-08) later Bishop of Peterborough. Ahead of us now is Petticoat Lane, Middlesex Street, which has been a street market for at least 400 years. Originally Hogs Lane because of the pigs kept in the fields there it soon became a clothes market, hence Peticote (1608), but in 1830 it was renamed Middlesex Street. It is still however known all over the world as Petticoat Lane and on Sundays hundreds of visitors come to buy goods of all kinds from a market which spills over into several local streets. In the 1550s 'the countryside was so foul and deep in the winter time that no man could pass by the same and in summer time men would not pass by the same for fear of infection by means of the filthiness that lay there.' A few years later Benedict Spinola, a wealthy Italian merchant, planted rows of elm trees and made the area more pleasant 'for citizens therein to walk, shoot and otherwise recreate and refresh their dulled spirits.'

Walking south we arrive at the Bar of the City marked by a dragon bearing the City Arms on a plinth. It was here that taxes and dues were paid before travellers passed through the Aldgate. It is advisable to cross the main road by the underpass and surface again in Aldgate High Street beside the Hoop and Grapes. Originally a thirteenth century inn, with overhanging upper storey and carved door posts and long narrow bar it reminds us of pre Fire Aldgate. The Haslemere Estates who recently restored it have produced an excellent history of the pub. Pevsner puts the building as c1690 but it may date from an earlier period. Also nearby is the Still and Star, another ancient inn probably commemorating the Star of Bethlehem over the stable and the Still providing another sort of spiritual succour.

Walking down Mansell Street we pass on the right the new Guinness Trust Housing developments of 1981 which are soon to be incorporated into the City of London. They can be approached by Haydon Street and Square, named after Captain John Haydon Lieutenant General of the Ordnance under Charles I who lived in the Minories. Sir Isaac Newton also lived here.

Goodmans Yard has recently become a busy one way road. Several streets and stiles were named after this seventeenth century farmer and the Goodmans Fields Theatres were famous in the eighteenth century. The Goodman family were of importance locally and the parish clerk always wrote their entries in the registers using exceptionally large characters. Marie daughter of William was buried on 20 February 1620 'in the night' and William's wife was buried four years later.

Pevsner reports that in 1787 a small Roman slab now in Burlington House was discovered here bearing the inscription, 'To the memory of Flavius Agricola, private in the Sixth Legion aged 42 years and 10 days.

11   Petticoat Lane

Erected by Albia Flavia to her peerless husband.' At the west end of
Goodman's Yard we turn left, walk under the railway and almost
immediately is Hammett Street which passes under the London Guildhall
University into The Crescent, recently rebuilt, where St Botolph's had its
vicarage. Behind this is a long piece of the old City Wall which can be
reached by a small gate and passage under the railway arch leading to
America Square so named because merchants trading with 'The Possessions'
lived here. None of the original 1770 houses designed by George Dance,
son of the architect of St Botolph's, survive. In 1836 the new London and
Blackwall Railway sliced off the southern part of the Square. Returning via
Crosswall to Minories we see Ibex House built in 1937 which Pevsner
describes as 'long bands of glass, whizzing round curved corners, the
Americans call the style Borax'. Just past it on the corner of St Clare Street
is the Three Lords pub which refers to Lords Kilmarnock, Balmerino and
Lovat who were the last people beheaded in the Tower – punished for
their part in Bonnie Prince Charlie's uprising in 1745. They are buried in
the Tower.

The area around St Clare Street (Church Street until 1929) is of great historic interest. It is the site of:

AD 91 - AD 268	A Roman burial ground
293 -1538	The Abbey of St Clare
1539 -1899	The Church of Holy Trinity, Minories rebuilt in 1568 and 1706 which stood at the eastern end of the street.
900 -1940	Parish Room of St Botolph's
1958 onwards	Office building at present owned by Pearl Assurance (Unit Funds) Ltd although the forecourt, formerly the graveyard, is owned by St Botolph's.

During the 1965 excavations of this site a coffin was unearthed whose breastplate revealed that it contained the remains of Anne Mowbray, child bride of one of the Princes in the Tower. This eight year old Duchess of York was probably buried here by her mother, the Duchess of Norfolk in 1481. Now she rests in Westminster Abbey close by the tiny skeletons found in the White Tower, 1674 and thought to be those of the two Princes who probably were murdered by their uncle, Richard III. Originally Anne had been buried in Westminster Abbey but the body was moved soon afterwards. My friend Dr Kevin McDonnell of Queen Mary College was the first person to find a sixteenth centuy manuscript in the British Museum recording this (see *East London Papers, July 1965*).

Returning to Minories we cross over into India Street and reach Jewry Street formerly The Poor Jewry inhabited mainly by Jews. On the eastern side stands the Sir John Cass building leased to the London Guildhall University. It was built in 1898 by A W Cooksey with an addition erected in 1934. Cooksey also designed the Primary School, 1910, which Pevsner describes as 'a cheerful neo Baroque, neo Hampton Court style with a central cupola.' At Aldgate High Street, opposite the church, is Portsoken House built to the design of Val Myers in 1928.

Sadly many old Aldgate buildings were destroyed by Hitler, City planners or plain neglect and it would be tiresome to list them all but mention must be made of the Three Nuns Inn which took its name from the Minoresses. It was a busy coaching inn of the 17th and 18th centuries and stood next to St Botolph's where Eagle Star have their offices today. It was rebuilt in 1877 as a hotel with eighty bedrooms and a facade fancifully designed in terracotta with stone dressings. It survived the Blitz but not the City developers and it came down in the late 1960s. Another famous tavern in Aldgate High Street was the Crown and Magpie pulled down in 1877 which made and exported its own beer. The nearby Boars Head, also destroyed, had a disreputable reputation as 'Lewde Playes' were to be seen there.

On our walk the eagle eyed might observe lead, shield shaped parish boundary marks 'SBA' affixed to buildings. Some are to be seen in Jewry Street.

Ghosts in Aldgate are rare but Jack Hallam in *Ghosts of London* (1975) mentions the Ghost of Aldgate Station which probably accounts for the disappearance of so many Circle Line trains. Footsteps and whistling are heard and in the 1960s an engineer saw an old man stroke the hair of one of his colleagues who was working on the high voltage equipment at the time. The man got two shocks at once but lived to tell the tale.

The graveyard of St Botolph's was at one time large and spacious, extending a good way to the north. This was sacrificed when the present St Botolph Street was built in the 1960s. On the west side of the church a few tombstones remain including one recalling the death of Thomas Ebrall, a Corn Merchant, shot by a Life Guardsman on 9 April 1850 in a local shop. He died eight days later. Shortly afterwards another tragedy occured when a gravedigger, Thomas Oates, and a young fish dealer, Edward Luddett, died from the fumes arising from a 'paupers grave where 18 bodies had been buried.' These were often left open until filled up and at the inquest the Alderman said he had complained about this to the Archdeacon but nothing had been done.

In 1742 the demolition of the old church revealed the fully clothed body of a 12 year old boy. 'The extraordinary circumstances of this boy is that his skin, fibres and intestines had all dried and very little of his bones appeared.' He weighed 18lbs. It was thought he had been shut in a vault at the time of the 1665 plague, the pits for which were dug to the north of the church.

On the outer wall of the churchyard is a drinking fountain erected to the memory of David Mocatta, 16 January 1905. Close by stood a large, heavy bronze statue of a cherub holding a paddle which was stolen in 1992. No one can explain how it could possibly have been lifted and carried away.

PART TWO
Challenges to the Church

9 HOMELESSNESS

George Appleton was a holy man whose books and *Daily Telegraph* articles have helped hundreds to pray, but he was not an otherworldly scholar. Far from it. In 1959 at the suggestion of Joost de Blank, Bishop of Stepney, he came to be interviewed as Rector by the churchwardens who asked him what he would do in his spare time as St Botolph's with its tiny congregation hardly warranted a full time priest. 'I'd like to make the church a centre for all religions,' said George and this warmed the heart of Bertie Hughes, churchwarden and owner of the Whitechapel Bell Foundry. 'I like ALL,' he said. 'We do not want someone who will make a beeline just for the Jews.' George got the job and soon built bridges with people of all faiths which stood him in good stead when he later became Archbishop of Jerusalem. When I visited him in September 1989 in Oxford to make notes about the crypt he said he was glad I continued his tradition. 'Never water down the faith to accommodate Jews or Muslims. It does you and them a disservice. They want to know what you believe and they respect you for saying it, so say it boldly and decisively.'

As nearly all the residents of Aldgate were Jewish, George set to work and visited many of them and sometimes they came to him to talk about family problems, drink or the sadness of bereavement. One Jewish visitor said to him, 'You Anglicans believe that the parish priest has some responsibility for everyone living in the parish. You are our Rector, so we want your comfort and advice from time to time, particularly if you do not press us to abandon our Jewish faith and culture.' In his autobiography George says this gave him a new vision of pastoral opportunity, 'for I could now see that if Christian clergy were prepared to be friendly and pastoral without any conditions or ulterior motives, the Christian Church could become a pastoral community provided it did not insist on claiming this responsibility or exploiting it.' He arranged a course of mid-week talks from Jewish rabbis and in the committee for Jewish work of which he was secretary, new ways of cooperation were discussed. A new name was adopted – The London Diocesan Council for Christian-Jewish Understanding, and St Botolph's is still its home and hosts an annual St Paul's lecture given alternately by Jewish and Christian scholars. Lecturers have included Lord Jakobovits, the Chief Rabbi, Donald Coggan, the Archbishop of York, Richard Harries, the Bishop of Oxford and Rabbi Lionel Blue.

Soon after his arrival George realised homeless men and women were gathering in the churchyard, many of whom were drunk on surgical spirits and in a very bad way. Their leader, Jimmy, suggested an evening canteen in the crypt which was full of old furniture and junk. There was only one clear space around the boiler. The coffins had long been removed although the floor was made up of gravestones laid somewhat precariously on brick foundations. Each morning the cleaner or the secretary, Leonora Hore, opened the church at 8am and as soon as George arrived from his flat in Shadwell Rectory people began begging money from him. Those who were in a hostel had been thrown out after breakfast so gathered in the church or yard. George realised something must be done and when the other churchwarden, a lawyer from Pinner, heard that the Rector wanted 'down and outs' in the crypt he said, 'For God's saky stop him.' George had wondered if a pensioners club would be more desirable but having found out that Toynbee Hall had a flourishing one he decided to turn the two eastern crypt tunnels into a daytime canteen for the homeless and accepting Jimmy's offer of help sent him each day to Leadenhall Market to beg or if necessary buy fruit and vegetables. The junk was cleared out, the grimy tunnel walls were whitewashed, posters were put up and the floor was made safe. Wash basins, lavatories and a bath were installed. Gordon Ventress, a retired army officer and lay reader, was paid a small sum to be in charge together with Harry King, a likeable, easy going grandfather who had once been a builder. George approached the GLC who gave a grant towards salaries but occasionally the cupboard was bare. On one worrying occasion George went down to the Mansion House to see the Lord Mayor who happened that year to be his old friend Bernard Waley-Cohen, Alderman of the Ward. Bernard listened gravely then sent for a clerk. 'How much do we give to good causes?'

'£25'

'How much do we give to really good causes?'

'£100'

George left with a cheque for £100.

Willie Samuel the Deputy of the Ward whose widow Iris is the present Deputy, also helped George raise money and in his autobiography *Unfinished* George recalls how his Jewish friends made no public appeal but drew up a list of people 'whom they thought would and could help and these were assessed by the organisers who said they knew quite well how much each ought to give with due regard to the circumstances at the time of asking, some of the necessary equipment being given in kind in preference to money.'

The curate and lecturer at this time was Nick Earle, a flamboyant and clever man with degrees from Oxford and Union Theological Seminary, New York, who taught in the Cass School and enjoyed writing books and speaking on Tower Hill. George occasionally was irritated by his criticisms so was amused when Nick was preaching once to a congregation including some of the inebriated crypt men. Nick began his sermon with his text, paused, then with a flourish repeated the text. 'I 'eard you the first time,' said Jimmy. George had particular affection for two other crypt users Oswald and Jesse who said they wanted to be married so George hired a room for them. Unfortunately Oswald was caught burgling a shop so the Rector went to see him in prison. 'Look after her for me Rev till I get out,' was the command. So George kept in touch. Just before Oswald's release he went to look for Jesse and found her very drunk in the Aldgate Arms having gone back to her old life as a prostitute. All the people in the bar listened to the Rector's pleading and shouted out, 'You go with the Rev, Jesse', so off they went arm in arm to Father Joe Williamson's hostel in Wellclose Square. George remembers they couldn't walk straight and fell over several times which considering he was wearing his dog collar must have amused passers by.

After a while a youth club was established in the other two tunnels of the crypt and for a time a weekly dance was held attended by members of both sides. Harry King changed his job and became the the full-time youth leader until 1968 when it closed.

Ken Leech, the distinguished theologian and preacher who joined the staff in 1990 recalls working in the crypt 1959-61 teaching English to Somalis when he was living with Fr Neville and the Franciscans in their Cable Street house.

Just after George Appleton left Aldgate to become Archdeacon of London he was scandalised to hear the police had raided the crypt and went to Bishopsgate police station to reproach the Inspector only to be told he had received a tip off about drugs. Trying to console George the Inspector said, 'We found no drugs and only one flick knife and one French letter.'

On Derek Harbord's arrival in 1962 things changed as his style was more formal than that of George. Conditions of employment were drawn up and formalised by the Parochial Church Council whom Derek reported to rather than consulted. Gordon Ventress, a keen Liberal supporter, absented himself from Derek's Induction in order to canvas for a by-election which shocked the ex-Judge. Soon afterwards Ventress left and after a short holding operation by Harry King, Derek asked Brother Richard Smith and Brother John Puttick of the Brotherhood of Prayer and Action to be in charge of the day work. The Brothers lived in the TocH hostel in Trinity

Square Minories which had formerly been the St Botolph's Rectory. Its warden Peter East had a particular interest in Bangladesh and was a great help to me with our youth club when I arrived at the church.

The evening work was staffed by volunteers coordinated by Leonard Taylor, a City businessman and by the churchwardens and treasurer. Sadly the day centre closed after a short time as the funding particularly from the St Martin in the Fields' fund dried up. The two Brothers left and their Order closed soon after.

Bobbie Beecroft, a secretary in the City and a woman of great charm and gentleness, took over from Len Taylor early in the 1970s and she was coordinating the volunteers for the four nights the crypt was open when I arrived in 1974. Trudie Eulenberg the parish worker played a large part because she was responsible for buying provisions and maintaining the premises. There was always much for her to do, with showers refusing to work, lavatories blocking, lights to be replaced and clothes to be taken in during the day. Bobbie had been a secretary at the London Hospital so had good administrative skills allied to patience and humour which I greatly appreciated. I owe her a lot because she realised I wanted to build on what had been achieved and never dampened my enthusiasm or said 'we don't do it that way'. She stayed for many years as volunteer coordinator and still visits occasionally.

In June 1973 Derek Harbord reported to his fellow governors of the Aldgate Freedom Foundation that their annual grant of £3,470 paid all the expenses of the centre which included a grant to the PCC of £960 for the services of Trudie, Peter the verger and a typist. Surprisingly the venture made a surplus of £387 even though £1,137 was spent on food. This is an interesting figure as in 1992 when numbers had increased five fold only £17,000 was spent on food thanks to the enormous amount of tins and provisions received at harvest time from our supporting parishes and schools. In 1976 I inserted an advert into *Church Times*, 'Dear Vicar, please send us your Harvest Goodies' and about 32 parishes responded. Today it is ten times that number and a marvellous partnership has grown up between the supporters and ourselves. The Revd Colin Midlane the counsellor and education worker until 1994 visited the parishes and schools in order to tell them how their gifts are used and help them understand the horrors of homelessness.

In 1973 the Centre's expenditure was £3,082. Twenty years later the expenditure of the crypt and hostels will be in the region of £1 million.

I was enormously impressed by the quality of Bobbie's volunteers who were City workers, students, housewives and all sorts of people. Shortly after my arrival I was showing a City historical group around the church and

David Hoffman

12   Waiting to get into the crypt, 1975

told them about the crypt work. 'We even have a brigadier washing lavatory floors but I haven't met him yet.' Afterwards a distinguished figure introduced himself as Brigadier John Packard and I felt very embarrassed. For the next 11 years he was to be one of our greatest supporters, getting us money from the Cripplegate Foundation and the City Social Services Department of which he was chairman. When I attended his crowded funeral at St Giles Cripplegate on 23 August 1993 I had a tremendous shock because this modest man had never told me he was a key figure in British Army Intelligence on staff work from before the second world war to the building of the Berlin Wall. He spoke Russian, French, Urdu, Hindi and Pashto fluently and before the war he had lived with a family in Berlin checking every garrison for troop movements, attending Nazi rallies, mixing with SS troops in order to discover the enemy's intentions. On retirement he moved from Suffolk to the City and began a new career of public service at the age of 61 which fortunately for us included a tremendous interest in St Botolph's.

The clothing store was a nightmare and caused me endless problems, so much so that after 12 years I closed it. Each day people would bring bags of old clothes which had to be stored somewhere. In the evenings in the south east corner of the crypt I would take up my position and throw open at 7 pm a sort of stable door. The crowd would surge forward and several times the 'door' had to strengthened to reject invaders. Customers were allowed in three at a time and I felt like an assistant in Harrods menswear department as I was told, 'these shoes are too small, or big, or narrow, or wide, or how do you expect me to get into this jacket?' We were once given a pair of enormous long johns and a volunteer and I were able to climb inside them, taking one leg each. When Gerald Ellison retired as Bishop of London he telephoned to tell me he had some old clothes for use in the crypt, so I said 'We don't have much call for copes and mitres'. He was not amused.

I put up a poster outside the church, 'Take off your clothes', which had the desired effect and several businessmen brought in old suits. George Foster one of the receptionists at Sedgwick House began to bring in huge parcels contributed by members of that firm who had moved into their new premises on our island site at the same time as I arrived. One of their senior directors, Michael Riesco and his wife Mollie, started a Steptoe project in Petworth where they lived so our clients benefited from some elegant town and country suiting. Sedgwicks seemed to enjoy our new friendship. I called on their chairman Neil Mills who arranged for a generous annual donation which still arrives, and David Brewer wrote the first of many articles about us for their glossy magazine edited by Wilton

Ashley and Muriel Musk. Joan Honeyman and Gwen Weller offered to publicise our events particularly our lunchtime talks amongst the 1,500 people working in their firm. Future chairmen, Carel Mosselman, Ian Findlay, Peter Wright and David Rowland (now chairman of Lloyds), continued to be generous to us and I arranged luncheon visits by Archbishop Coggan and Archbishop Runcie to the firm. I shall always be grateful to Carel because he gave short shift to an evangelical member of the firm who asked him to break links with us because we supported liberal causes. 'When the bishop sacks Malcolm I might listen to you,' he said. 'Not until then.'

I felt it was vitally important that all the religious agencies working in the single homeless field in East London cooperate to avoid duplication of services. The local authorities seemed uninterested so the Providence Row Sisters of Mercy (RC), Bow, Whitechapel and Cable Street Missions (Methodist), the large Petticoat Lane and Whitechapel Road hostels (Salvation Army) and Spitalfields Crypt (Anglican) joined St Botolph's to form 'No Fixed Abode'. I was given the task of preparing a leaflet explaining our work and I decided to do it in a question and answer form. Unfortunately despite my pointing it out at proof stage the replies to two questions were muddled up: 'Who are the helped? – business men, housewives, students and others. Who are the helpers? – mainly middle aged men of whom many have a drink problem or history of mental illness and violence.'

I was visited a few days before my first Christmas by a *Times* reporter who came hotfoot from being with bankers and dealers. He seemed shocked by what he described as the smell of urine and feet in the crypt but impressed by my rather cavalier statement that we believed our visitors were valuable and could be full human beings again. He interviewed Nick Alder, a nineteen year old volunteer from the City Polytechnic Accountancy Department, who said he had initially been revolted by what he had seen but was now a committed helper. The reporter commented 'I saw a girl holding the hand of an incoherent drunk for half an hour smiling the whole time. One or two of the customers are painfully respectable persons carefully though shabbily dressed who are there because they are hungry. Many of the regulars look sullen. One woman noisily dismantled a bag in which to put sandwiches for her mates. A small Indian nun, one of Mother Theresa's order, smiled and said quietly, Ssh, I'll find you a bag.'

I soon realised that volunteers could not provide continuity from one evening to another no matter how committed they were. The day work had ceased several years earlier so what they needed was a full time

13   The crypt canteen, 1975

member of staff to help. Where could I find such a person? Thanks to the suggestion of an old friend Canon Richard Eckersley I approached the Church Army whose work I had no knowledge of. Over the next fifteen years they provided some outstanding workers: Terry Drummond, Keri Deasy, Jerry Sugg, Aidan Webster and now Lee Willis. Terry with Linda his wife arrived in 1975 and I told them I expected great things from them. They were to live in the flat at the top of Whitechapel Post Office recently vacated by the formidable Archdeacon of Hackney Michael Hodgins. Terry soon set to work and a shop front was established in the crypt for advice, particularly on alcohol problems. Contacts were slowly built up with organisations which could help but more importantly the men who came to the crypt began to make friends with Terry and trust him. 'We don't push them to stop drinking', said Terry, 'because we believe that they must make the decision, but we do offer support when the decision has been made.' Alcohol has always been a major problem in the crypt so it is good that later we were able to employ especially trained workers in the field, such as Katrina Herbert. We made a rule that men and women would be admitted to the crypt smelling of alcohol but no bottles would be allowed and no one exhibiting aggressive behaviour could be welcomed.

I knew I must formulate a strategy to fight the obscenity of homelessness and in my mind I drew up five headings.

Immediate needs

The evening canteen was the first – a place where anyone could be welcomed and given immediate help and friendship. We had several discussions about charging for food and several people felt this would help people budget their income and stand on their own two feet. I resisted this idea strongly because although most of our visitors would be able to budget, a significant number who were mentally unstable or socially inadequate could not and I did not want them turned away. In 1974 there were about 70 people each evening. Today the numbers have risen to 200-300 of whom perhaps 5-10 per cent are not able to jump through the financial hoops we would erect. The immediate needs for food, washing facilities, laundry, clothes, were all met by our growing number of staff and volunteers. Fabian Moynihan who had been a Franciscan Friar, joined the staff in 1977 and was an invaluable helper who always seemed to be in several places at once.

14　Art class at the day centre, 1990

Long term help

The second front in the war against homelessness was the Day Centre which was established in 1981. Evening numbers were now overwhelming so a smaller group was needed which could meet during the day cared for mainly by paid workers skilled in counselling. To begin with we had two entirely separate staff teams which meant the left hand never knew what the right hand was doing so this idea was abandoned and one team, presided over by a new senior social worker Daly Maxwell, set to work. St Botolph's owes a large debt to Daly who created a warm, loving, accepting atmosphere in the day and evening centres. An hour long TV programme made in 1990 revealed the depth of his commitment and showed what a magnificent worker and leader he is. In 1993 he moved to a new job in Brighton.

The day centre cares for up to forty women and men with a carefully structured programme of classes, discussions, outings etc and a shared meal at lunchtime when workers, visitors and supporters all mingle together. It was here that I had some of the best conversations about art, (with those who had been attending Liz Ellis's Art Class), theology, literature and politics. The exhibitions of painting, prose and poetry mounted by the day centre are always impressive. Regular holidays are arranged with the Hoppers Hospital in Kent and if the necessary skilled volunteers are around swimming and gymnasium outings are fixed. The police cadets from Hendon Training School who come for six week placements are useful with this and also at breaking down the barriers many of us put up against the police force. Other placement students come for two month periods from hospitals, theological colleges and social work courses. Each year we employ three people for twelve months so we learn from them and they learn from us. Several of our staff have been ordained including Jonathan French, David Palmer, Michael Taylor, Roger Kent, Pam Wise, Elaine Jones, Martin Smith, Louis Newton, Andy Delmege and Hugh Rayment Pickard. Thanks to their time in the Centre these ministers have knowledge of homelessness which few of their fellow clergy share.

In the day centre each visitor has a key worker and much progress is made with getting accommodation or jobs or helping them regain self respect. At the end of each day a tea party is held at which everyone says how they feel about the day and sometimes this can be very moving particularly when someone leaves. When I myself left St Botolph's the tea party in a tunnel of the crypt was extremely painful and I was in tears as people spoke about the work I had done and sang some songs and gave me presents. Daly and his team had a marvellous gift of creating community under ground, and this tradition continues.

Education

So many people even our own supporters have odd ideas about homeless people, saying 'They want to be homeless, they enjoy it, they should pull themselves together and get a job.' Ten minutes in the crypt which included meeting someone on the streets or living in a hostel soon disabused them of that. We welcome visitors from parishes or schools provided they are not 'looking at the animals.' I tried to persuade the church authorities to let me have St Ethelburga or St Katharine Cree church to be a centre of urban studies but my pleas fell on deaf ears. I wanted somewhere to take groups and show them the issues involved before they visited the crypt, the afterwards ask them to share impressions. Perhaps the new plans for city Churches might incorporate this idea for St Katharine Cree.

The causes of homelessness are complicated and varied because usually a combination of events will push a person downwards – the loss of a job, the death or divorce of a spouse, mental inadequacy or instability, a tendency to alcohol or drugs. Rarely but sometimes it may be laziness. As Pat Logan has pointed out in *A Life to be Lived* the world of a homeless person is one of shrinking horizons because the ordinary world has collapsed. Once your home is gone close personal friendships can soon disappear and nothing seems to have purpose anymore. Life is telescoped into getting through the next 24 hours so you queue for hours in impersonal cold offices to get money or you beg. You have nowhere to wash yourself or your clothes. Doors, even church doors, are closed in your face and people avoid you. 'Homelessness is not merely the absence of a home anymore than poverty is a lack of cash. It is the collapse of a world, the withdrawal of all security and the destruction of personal relationships.' Pat knows what he is writing about.

Education is therefore an important part of the crypt's work and I am glad that with its slides and videos it is now a resource place for Christians and others to learn about a neglected part of our city life. It is vital for staff and volunteers to share their experience, to act as a voice for the voiceless, but also to encourage the homeless to speak for themselves. Fortunately this is now happening and the magazine *The Big Issue* as well as providing an income for people on the streets helps the well heeled understand what society is doing to some of its members.

Somewhere to live

The provision of accommodation is the fourth front I wanted to work on in the battle against homelessness. In 1978 I was standing in the church kitchen when Philip Corby, the Master of the Belltower, called in to tell me he had been part of a deputation which had visited Prince Philip to ask him to be patron of the World of Property Housing Association on whose council Philip sat. The Prince had asked what the Association was doing about homelessness and what if anything were they doing in East London where they had recently purchased a long lease of the Sir John Cass Estate in Hackney – some six hundred properties. Philip had been deputed to come and see me, so his question, 'Do you want a hostel' was thrilling beyond words. I met Alan Bailey the Director of the Association and soon afterwards I was a member of their London Committee. The Chairman, Edward Erdman, the founder of an international practice of property consultants and surveyors which bears his name, was very enthusiastic and when I established a new charity 'The Lodge Project' to build hostels he became a trustee and rarely missed a meeting. Now in his mid eighties he retains a special concern for the homeless poor and his book *People and Property* describes his long eventful life. His advice and financial help were invaluable.

It was at this time that I met Hilda Bazalgette who was also a member of the Association's Council. She became deputy chairman of the Lodge Project. A formidable lady who died in 1993 she always wore an elegant hat and was known to everyone as Dame Hilda. Educated at Girton, Cambridge she had been general secretary of the National Association of Women Civil Servants for nineteen years and in the forefront of women's fight for equal opportunities. Mark Cato and his successor as director of the Association, Mike Annan, were other trustees together with the nominations from St Botolph's PCC, Tim Mills, Billy Dove, Michael Wilson and Glen Coleman. Hackney Council nominated Councillor Joanne Andrews, and we coopted Dr Greta Foster of the London Hospital and Lynne Brooke and David Dawes, City lawyers.

Planning the new hostel (to be named Park Lodge), in Victoria Park Road proved to be a nightmare as the local Residents Association decided to try and stop it. I went to one of their meetings held in a large hall and was harangued by a huge crowd of people shouting at me like fish wives. They accused me of building on parkland (the derelict bomb site on the edge of the park had in fact been built on pre-war) and bringing to their residential area vagrants who would attack the elderly and seduce children. I was vary badly shaken by the experience and was particularly angry that they had refused me a fair hearing. Their Association collapsed soon after and fortunately Hackney Council, taking no notice of them, granted planning permission. I had been careful to involve the local councillors and the staff of the Social Services Department so our relations with the Borough were good.

Having had no experience whatsoever in furnishing a hostel I relied very heavily on Barbara Branford a friend from Raynes Park who joined the management committee. Early on I decided not to accept second hand furniture, crockery, linen etc as I wanted the rooms to look good and be of a high standard. John Lewis's offered a generous discount which meant each bedsit had a beautifully furnished kitchen, bathroom and living room. Many of the rooms looked across parkland.

Two months before the official opening of Park Lodge disaster struck. Early one morning a fire broke out in the roof and a few mornings later another fire damaged the stairs. The police were convinced it was arson and that one of the twenty two residents was responsible. The warden, Les O'Dell, and his assistant David Kirk joined me in interviewing all the residents. An expert in the psychology of arsonists had sent me some information to help catch the culprit but we failed to do so . A few days before the official opening another larger fire destroyed the common room where we were to have tea. Near to tears I phoned Miss Mona Mitchell the private secretary to HRH Princess Alexandra who was to be our guest of honour. She spoke to the Princess who said that she would still like to come as obviously our morale needed a boost. I had to act quickly as we could no longer have refreshments at the Lodge so I walked to a nearby nightclub, Goochi's, and saw the two owners who were brothers. Straightway they offered their rooms free of charge, so on 15 February 1984 on a bright sunny afternoon we welcomed the Princess to Park Lodge where she unveiled a plaque, met the architect, the trustees and 22 residents, then with the Bishops of London and Stepney she joined sixty further guests for tea provided by the ladies of the nearby parish, St John of Jerusalem. It was a splendid occasion and the Princess spoke to everyone present. Soon afterwards I had the terrible task of moving all the residents to other hostels knowing that one of them was an arsonist. At the same time we decided that we would change the client group so that we could still house homeless men and women but one third would be physically handicapped, one third mentally disturbed and one third socially disadvantaged. Economically this was better for us as we would have a larger income and then could employ more staff. Two ground floor rooms were adapted for wheelchair use and a lift was installed. Residents stay for one or two years and are then enabled by the resettlement team to move into their own flats nearby if possible. Pat Peart who became Coordinator of Park Lodge in August 1988 is a woman of great experience who with Andrew Law has made Park Lodge a place of excellence and a model of good practice which meant that the BBC featured the work in a TV documentary in 1993.

New Islington and Hackney Housing Association offered us a house in

David Hoffman

15   Moving into new accommodation

Graham Road to be our second Lodge. Having learnt so much from the Park Lodge experience we asked Barbara Townley to prepare carefully for the arrival of the nine residents who live in the two flats. We named it Littlewick Lodge to honour one of the supporting parishes in the Oxford diocese and the Lord Mayor of London Sir Christopher Collett and the Lady Mayoress performed the ceremony in June 1989. Another hostel, Scott Lodge, quickly followed for three men affected by the HIV virus cared for by a part-time worker, James Allen. A further hostel, for eleven people was opened in association with the City Corporation and named after Philip Corby who died in 1992.

The Housing Minister, Sir George Young, paid a visit to see how we were spending his generous Department of Environment grant and said he was most impressed by the business like, caring atmosphere of Park Lodge and promised to help if he could with any further housing projects.

Politics

Campaigning was the last of the five items on my agenda. One of the reasons why I have been on the General Synod is to speak there on issues concerning homelessness and health. Few listen to these speeches so in 1991 I was delighted when Fr Ken Leech joined the staff. As a theologian, writer and excellent communicator he is able to share our experience with others by speeches, seminars, articles and books.

We felt it important that he does his theology at parish level and helps us to think theologically about the work upstairs and downstairs in St Botolph's.

Larger staff and premises

As the numbers of people coming to St Botolph's for help increased by leaps and bounds we had to employ a much larger staff and it soon became apparent that our premises needed modernising and extending. The first stage was to take over the whole crypt so the youth club was closed in 1979 and plans were made to create one unit with a kitchen, meeting rooms and offices. We were fortunate in being given a Sunday morning BBC Radio 4 Week's Good Cause, which I did myself and about £30,000 poured in. Morgan Williams an old friend produced it and gave me lots of hints about how to use the four minutes available. A very generous business man in Herefordshire telephoned to ask how much our annual electricity bill was and put a cheque in the post to cover it. A month later George Goodsir of the stockbrokers Brewin Dolphin sent me the good news that the same donor wanted St Botolph's to have a share portfolio worth £30,000. We could hardly believe it and since then Mr Goodsir has increased the value of the gift by careful management. It was a tremendous help for me to know this security existed and only once did I have to raid it when we had no other means of paying salaries.

In the mid 1980s we decided to build an extension to the east of the church by filling in the dirty, Dickensian yard where our visitors had to wait for opening time protected only by a lean-to covered way. The Harbord Memorial as we called the outside lavatory, (he named it Clochmerle) had to be pulled down and John Phillips our architect designed a spacious meeting room lit from above, offices, counselling rooms and a new much needed medical centre. The Department of Health after much lobbying agreed to replace our splendid volunteer doctors and nurses who had included Dr Hugh John, the City's Medical Officer of Health, by paid staff who would regard us as a National Health surgery for the Homeless. We were even promised an annual rent. A public appeal was launched in May 1985 by Leslie Crowther who showed great knowledge of homelessness and we had a splendid late afternoon reception in the Mansion House. A BBC TV appeal followed which raised £90,000. The centre spoke for itself with a commentator describing how the hundreds of people who come through the doors are helped. It was a very humbling experience opening the thousands of letters all of which received a reply from me. This was organised by Leslie Bridgeman our appeal coordinator who had to work from a desk in the side chapel of the church as there was no room in the crypt for him. Methodical and efficient, he sent hundreds of appeal letters and logged all donations. Some letters were very moving indeed – several were marked 'a gift from an OAP who values her warm home'; one lady sent us her wedding ring to sell; many pound coins were wrapped in messages of hope and love. The prize letter came from Gorleston on Sea where a gentleman told us he had enjoyed seeing Sarah our social worker on the screen in the TV appeal, would like to marry her and enclosed the times of the buses from Aldgate to Great Yarmouth. The new large meeting room was named The Hunter Room after Fr John Hunter who had recently died – and the new extension was opened by the Lord Mayor of London on 22 September 1987.

All this building work was master minded by Richard Basch, our able administrator from 1982-93 who also drew up the plans for the new hostels. His next challenge was clearing the vault under the church steps which contained huge piles of bones and about thirty five coffins dating from the beginning of the nineteenth century. All were in a terrible state of decomposition so I decided the dead must make way for the living.

Thanks to a generous grant from the City Churches Grants Committee, supported by Archdeacon Cassidy, we engaged a firm rejoicing in the splendid name Necropolis Ltd to move the six thousand skeletons to Canning Town Cemetery. A marble headstone now marks the spot where they were reburied. Remarkable funereal looking operatives dug the bones out of the lime soil, packed them into plastic bags and loaded them into vans early in the morning. One man slept in a caravan on the site to guard it against undesirable peeping toms. Whilst they were burrowing they discovered an entrance to yet another vault which is under the small piece of garden between St Botolph's and the Eagle Star building. I could face no further building work so the entrance was bricked up.

Further money was needed for this extension building but this time I did not launch a public appeal but depended on our generous supporters. The ITV Sunday Evening Appeal was another success raising £120,000, some of which was used to install a lift in Park Lodge. Sir Peter Miller, former chairman of Lloyds, brought fifty of the staff of Thomas Miller Ltd, Jewry Street, to see the new work and handed me a cheque for £40,000! I realised how very lucky we are to have so many friends in the business houses locally. Also present was Richard Briers who had given up a great deal of time to appear in the ITV appeal for us. He was seen talking to several of our visitors and there is no doubt that the huge sum received was largely due to his popularity.

I was particularly pleased when we began to get government funding although once it caused much havoc. I was told by the Greater London Council that a grant of £40,000 had been agreed and I would receive the cheque shortly. Six weeks later when our bank balance looked precarious I telephoned twice and an official told me the grant had been paid and the cheque cleared. Richard Basch our administrator and I checked all the accounts and found nothing so Richard telephoned again to be told we must be a useless, inefficient organisation to mislay such a large amount of money. More checking of all church and crypt accounts revealed nothing. Then I suddenly remembered that when I visited GLC Headquarters on the South Bank our file had been next to one marked 'St Botolph Aldersgate' so I telephoned the priest in charge of that church and asked if he had received a cheque from the GLC. 'Oh yes,' he said, 'It's absolutely marvellous, we have a public appeal for our Tower and quite out of the blue, unasked for, the GLC sent £40,000. We have started to spend it.' My next call was to the official at GLC who seemed shocked at my forceful language and a cheque arrived the next day. Sadly, Aldersgate had to return their gift.

Over £1 million has been raised for these extensions to our crypt which means the quality of the service we offer to our visitors improved immeasurably. The kitchen and showers needed modernising so before I left in 1992 I had one more final heave at money raising and, ably assisted by Brother Jude SSF, another £200,000 arrived.

The visit of Princess Alexandra on 27 February 1992 was the culmination of all this activity. A Service of Thanksgiving was held in the church during which three people attending the crypt spoke publicly with our curate, Nerissa Jones, about their experiences of being homeless. The Princess and her Lady in Waiting were much moved and later found a job for one of the three. At the reception afterwards we remembered all that had been done in the Crypt since George Appleton opened the centre thirty years before.

Some crypt characters

The mobile x-ray unit which scans for TB, pays regular visits to St Botolph's and usually staff and visitors are x-rayed. After one such visit Jim who lived in a disused building with his dog Mitch, received a letter at the church asking him to go into the London Chest Hospital as soon as possible, so in a foolish moment I offered to care for Mitch whom I installed in the Battersea Dogs Home. Jim was in hospital longer than expected so the costs at Battersea began to mount up. Then I remembered Mrs Curtis, mother of one of our congregation, who lives in a prefab in Hackney with 35 stray cats and 6 dogs. I went to see her and when I had moved ten cats off the settee and sat down I explained the situation. 'Bring him here,' she said and that afternoon a rather terrified, disorientated Mitch joined the circus. He stayed for four weeks and every Sunday afternoon Mrs Curtis took him to the lawn outside the hospital ward and Jim would wave out of the window to Mitch who would wave back.

One morning a very scrawny hen with her feathers ruffled walked up the front steps of the church and came in – she had obviously fallen off a lorry bound for the Petticoat Lane slaughter house. Much discussion took place about her future and eventually compassion linked with her obvious inedibility meant we took her to Stepping Stones Farm, Stepney for rehabilitation. She seemed pleased.

Mr Swift's battered trilby was always on at a jaunty angle. He rarely spoke but was always in the evening centre propped up by his crutches in a corner. No one knew when his leg had been amputated, perhaps he was one of the many war veterans in the crypt. He slept in doorways or skips and one Christmas we were horrified to discover he had been beaten up as he slept in our blankets at the door of the Centre. We all had a special affection for him as his photograph showing Bobbie Beecroft cutting his hair had appeared on one of our brochures. Daly knew Mr Swift liked the countryside and asked him if he would agree to live in a farm hostel for older men in Yorkshire. To our surprise he agreed, so smartened up by Doris Boyds's second hand clothing department he accompanied Daly on an Inter City train to Yorkshire. Five years later we still miss him and often wonder if he is making his way back to London down the A1.

Keri Deasy obviously had a special care for the women visitors who were heavily outnumbered by the men and a room was created for them in the Centre and Lucy Firth extended these facilities. Forty year old Hilda a regular visitor was loud mouthed, tall and a nuisance to everyone upstairs and downstairs. Gradually Keri made friends with her and weaned her off alcohol and found her a flat to live in with Min her kitten. It was a success story. When she was on the streets Keri was worried at her medical condition and she was admitted to the London Hospital for a hysterectomy. Visiting her, propped up by pillows and all clean and fragrant was an experience as her conversation could be heard several wards away. As I blessed her then kissed her goodbye she said, 'Malc, you smell like a gardenia.'

Only twice in eighteen years was I frightened of physical violence in the crypt. Soon after my arrival I was on the stairs leading to my study when a huge man pounced on me and I ran for help. The hairs on the back of my neck stood up. Just before I left St Botolph's I was in the doorway between the TV room and the kitchen when a very aggressive man ran at me to hit me. With great presence of mind a volunteer fortunately shut the door in his face. Usually the other visitors would come to the help of anyone under threat and part of the training for staff and volunteers was learning the art of talking oneself out of trouble and signalling for help. In 1990 we bought some tiny portable alarms which if pressed rang bells at three central points in the building. Fortunately physical and verbal abuse are not common and we agreed a policy which means that a prosecution is brought if people are hurt or buildings damaged.

At one time the congregation included a nineteen year old man who dressed in morning suit and carried a cane. He timed his entrance to cause maximum disturbance – usually five minutes after the Service began or in the middle of the sermon. He would walk down the centre aisle, enter the front pew, clattering his stick on the bench or floor, lift his tails to reveal a non too clean shirt, turn to look at his fellow worshippers then sit down. He lived in squalor with his mother in a large Victorian house, she in the cellar, he on the top floor. We managed to get him into a hostel and soon he began a course at the FE College. He continued to dress occasionally in morning clothes and one Sunday another worshipper appeared in a wedding dress looking like Miss Havisham. On the steps after the Service they made a handsome pair, and passers by thought a wedding had taken place.

10 THE TIGHTROPE WALKER

St Botolph's concern for gay and lesbian people

'Malcolm will never get preferment, he has taken certain pastoral initiatives.'

Fr Percy Coleman

The circumstances of my appointment to St Botolph's were very odd. The Bishop of London, Robert Stopford, whom I visited three times at Fulham Palace before his retirement in 1973 had several conversations with me about the pastoral care of homosexuals, because I had put forward a plan which would enable me to be based at a central London church in order to visit gay pubs and clubs and be an unofficial chaplain to this particular scene. The Bishop, a friendly, pipe-smoking down to earth family man had listened to me, seen the need, and in two letters promised to help. Sitting in his study I took a deep breath and told him that since the law had changed in 1967 I and several other counsellors of the Albany Trust were concerned that the three million or so homosexuals in this country should no longer be treated as second or third class citizens by the Church, the State, or by society at large. As a priest I was particularly concerned that those who were Christians should put their faith and their sexuality together. I told him I had counselled several hundred people over the years and had blessed gay unions which were not marriages but the couples believed their love was divine in origin and wanted to affirm that love in church. I had always thought that if clergy can bless battleships and budgerigars we could bless two people in love. My experience had taught me that homosexual men and women could form deep loving relationships but so much was stacked against them. He agreed that many Christians seemed particularly hostile so perhaps I could build a few bridges between gay people and the Church. In fact I already had made a tentative start with two friends Andrew Henderson and Christopher Spence, by founding a Saturday night social group where people could relax and meet each other. This still survives at St Katharine's 25 years later and many hundreds of people have used the group to come to terms with their sexuality and to make friends.

Bishop Robert tried twice to get me a base for this work but his retirement overtook everything. Before leaving Fulham he burnt all my personal files which contained letters and notes of our conversations but he left a message for his successor 'Malcolm needs a City Living'. When Bishop Gerald Ellison came from Chester to London he wrote to me in February 1974 offering me a City Living – St Botolph's, Aldgate. I remember standing in the Chaplaincy to Queen Mary College in the Mile End Road reading and rereading the letter, hardly able to believe my luck.

The Bishop, a distinguished, handsome, patrician figure with a voice to match did not interview me on my acceptance and all seemed well. Two weeks before the Induction Fr John Hester now a Canon Residentiary of Chichester went to see Bishop Gerald about his parish of Soho and as he left the study let slip, 'I'm glad you have appointed Malcolm to St Botolph's, he can now get on with his work.' 'What work?' asked the Bishop. Fr John realised he had let the cat out of the bag but was wise enough not to try to stuff it back in. So he described the work I wished to do and the Bishop made no comments then or at the Induction. However, a few months later when he came for Confirmation he tackled me at the lunch party which followed in my house. He took me into the dining room, sat me down, lamented he had no file on me and asked my plans, so I described the work I had in mind but said that St Botolph's was not a quiet City church with nothing to do so the time available would be limited. The Bishop looked apprehensive.

Then began a long succession of letters back and forth from London House beginning 'My dear Bishop' 'My dear Malcolm'. I have them still and they make interesting reading because all the Bishop's comments about the many controversial issues raised are courteous and wise and replies came usually by return.

Six months after my Induction I became very concerned that homosexual Christians felt estranged from the mainline churches and were flocking to their own gay church, the Fellowship of Christ the Liberator, meeting in West London, – an English branch of the Metropolitan Community Church in the States which was founded by Troy Perry specifically for gay and lesbian Christians.

It seemed to me then, and still does now, that as we do not have special churches for left handed people, those with auburn hair or those over six foot tall, homosexuals should not have their own separate denomination. One way of integrating them would be to offer the use of St Botolph's to the young minister of the Fellowship, Tom Bigelow who turned out to be an Episcopalian priest, so I had several talks with Tom and he asked me to write for a reference to his bishop in the States. In January 1975 I had a letter from the Rt Revd Ivol Ira Curtis, Bishop of Olympia, saying Tom was a pleasant fellow and a fine priest but he, the bishop, had 'no

was glad the Movement was behaving responsibly but could not resist a complaint that the word gay had a new meaning which now made it difficult for him to use it in 'ordinary parlance.'

When I wanted to employ as a successor to David Randall our Youth Chaplain a talented priest who was then working as a child care officer, Gerald asked Bishop Mark Hodson to interview him. The man was living with a male partner which greatly disturbed Bishop Hodson and he vetoed the plan. I found this strange as Hodson had been surrounded by gay clergy for much of his ministry so I wrote to express my objection saying a partnership nearly always gives stability to a homosexual priest. I was very disappointed and not a little angry with Bishop Hodson. At the same time Edwyn Young, a flamboyant former Rector of Stepney and friend of Hodson whom he resembled (both married late in life) told a young priest considering joining our team he should not touch us with a bargepole. I regarded this as a great tribute, and told him so a few years later when we met at a church function.

In the summer of 1978 I at last realised I could not do all the counselling work needed for the many people who were coming for help. For three Christmasses we had put on a Carol Service for the homosexual community in London which was always packed to the doors. This together with a Service for Gay Pride Week in the summer and all our various contacts had meant many gays and lesbians were seeing us as a resource place for worship, prayer, counselling and friendship. I had also established a meeting twice a year for homosexual clergy (someone suggested I should hire the Albert Hall) and this had meant clergy as well as laity were seeking us out so I needed to find a talented priest with counselling skills. I remembered an ordinand whom I had met at Ripon Hall some years before so I telephoned him in Wales. John Lee had been a research scientist in Australia before ordination and was now at St Teilo's Porthead. He came to see me and my initial thoughts were confirmed because he had all the necessary gifts together with a good sense of humour and a marvellous gentle generous spirit.

I realised Gerald would not approve of this sort of counselling work so I devised a job specification which looked as though John would be setting up a hostel and doing counselling work occasionally where as in fact there was little hostel work to do as Park Lodge, our first hostel, would not open for another four years. John wanted a rest from parish life so we employed him as a member of the crypt staff which meant he did not need a Licence to officiate, which was just as well as Gerald refused to give one. He only agreed a year later when people like Bishop Kenneth Woolcombe and others in London who had seen the high quality of John's work lobbied him. John married Sue shortly after his arrival in London and they now have three children, Joseph, Rebecca and Sophie. Their home has been a refuge for countless people in need and they have been extraordinarily generous to me and many others. John completed his training at the Institute of Group Analysis, stayed at St Botolph's six years and now works part time at Bart's Hospital as well as being Rector of Chiddingstone in Kent. It was a good move having a heterosexual counsellor available for homosexuals although he tells me he occasionally had to cope with clients who expected more than counselling. It also showed that there is no reason why a non gay person should not counsel gays, as John is one of the most talented and compassionate men I have met.

The Gloucester Report which discussed the Christian attitude to homosexuality was published in the Autumn of 1979 and I wrote to my Bishop telling him how disappointed I was at its contents. No openly homosexual person sat on the Commission and I felt their treatment of gays and particulary those in committed relationships was 'a gross insult'. I pointed out that I had been counselling homosexuals for over ten years had recently made a study of 87 couples I knew personally and in my experience the Report had treated them unfairly and would now, with its suggestion that gay loving was second class, make my ministry to them much more difficult. Anyone branded second rate is tempted to behave in a second rate way and might well consider leaving the Church. Back came a six sided reply in his own handwriting. He felt anything he said particularly in public would be misunderstood and made the distinction between being gay and doing something about it. He felt my point of view was so far removed from the standards of Christian teaching as to be unacceptable to the majority of Christian people. The Church could never condone sodomy; celibacy must be embraced, said Bishop Gerald, 'I cannot believe that our generation has been vouchsafed some understanding of the issues denied to our forefathers or that we have any right to cast aside the traditional teaching of the Church.' I replied on 8 November 1979 saying that the vital component missing from the discussion was experience and that the Church must now face the diversity and complexity of human sexuality. We had to agree to disagree. It was made more poignant by the fact that I had never discussed my own personal situation with him, although, in an earlier conversation, he had mentioned a Canon of St Paul's who lived with his friend, commending them for their discretion. Why could I not follow their example? When I later told the Canon about the conversation he was scandalised. 'How does he know? Who told him?'

The Queen visited St Botolph's in March 1980 and Gerald got drawn into the controversy as to whether her eyes would be soiled by seeing

LGCM pamphlets on our bookstall. He asked who the authors were and I told him- Fr Harry Williams CR, Kennedy Thom the chaplain of Essex University and Sara Coggin, a teacher. He made no comments and was not bothered by a report in *Private Eye* about 'the club for homosexuals in St Botolph's crypt' which was totally untrue. He said he had seen the magazine in the House of Lords Library, rarely read it, and counselled I should ignore it. I did.

Bishop Gerald resigned later that year and I was sad to see him go. At his City farewell in what turned out to be a prophetic speech he said a retired person had three thoughts. 'What a strange person they have chosen to succeed me, what a mess he is making and, does it matter anyway?'

After leaving London Gerald was asked by Robert Runcie to care for the troubled diocese of Bermuda; following that he settled with his wife, Jane in Cerne Abbas where he had a particular ministry amongst retired clergy. He died in October 1992 having been a bishop for 44 years and in *The Independent* obituary Alan Webster saluted a man, trained as an oarsman and naval chaplain who never rocked the ecclesiastical boat. He was, Alan says, 'so confident in his own powers of leadership that he could afford to make daring appointments – Donald Reeves to St James' Piccadilly, Malcolm Johnson to Aldgate and Gonville French Beytagh to St Vedast's Foster Lane. He searched for individuals committed to the community rather than to churchy trivia.'

I felt a great sense of sadness at his passing as he had always respected if not agreed with me and I felt warmed by the fact that he several times asked me to be his chaplain at the November Service of Remembrance in the Albert Hall, and twice asked me to preach in St Paul's Cathedral.

I missed Bishop Gerald because from then on I received little guidance and support from his successor, Graham Leonard. Letters were rarely answered and when I was granted an interview the bishop did most of the talking about himself. He chose me to be Area Dean 1985-90, after two others had declined it, but consulted me no more than five times in five years and I can only recall three telephone conversations about City affairs in all that time. Area Deans meetings were a farce – dashing through the Diocesan Directory discussing clergy in a very superficial way and avoiding all the real issues. Policy or strategy for the London Area was never discussed. Bishop Graham also had a habit of trying to put me in my place by beginning every conversation with, 'I've had a letter of complaint about you.' Bishop Gerald on the other hand once told me that he could tell who the best priests of his Diocese were because they had the fattest files in the filing cabinet.

The new bishop visited St Botolph's on 13 November 1981 for the Service of Thanksgiving for the Crypt re-ordering and redecoration during which Alison Limerick, the well known black dancer and singer whose mother Sarah worships at St Botolph's, danced before the altar, and Rabbi Lionel Blue spoke in the service. Graham said the Service was 'glorious, both dignified and relaxed.' The following Spring he visited the Crypt and I showed him the offending pamphlets on the bookstall. He like myself thought them useful for adult discussion but boring and unreadable for children. The ambiguity of Bishop Graham's attitude to me meant I was always confused in my relationship with him. He appeared to be supportive but made no attempt to talk at depth with me about my concerns nor did he try to stop the confrontations which were to come. Many thought he himself was the architect of the troubles.

My appointment as Area Dean of the City brought Graham some hassle because he received objections from Basil Watson, the right wing Rector of St Lawrence Jewry, the Corporation's church and also from the Evangelical Rector of St Helen's Bishopsgate Dick Lucas and seven of his senior men in the congregation. I went to see Basil who was under the mistaken impression I had organised the demonstration by men in skirts which had disrupted the talk by Mrs Whitehouse in his church some weeks earlier. I was unaware the lady had visited the City, but Basil declined to join in any City Deanery events whilst I was Dean, which brought no tears to my eyes as he had once told me not to be 'insolent' at a meeting of the Sion College Court of Governors. Dick Lucas and I had a long discussion about the authority of Scripture which revealed that we had totally different ideas of Authority in the Church of England. I quoted Bible, Church and Reason and for an hour we unsuccessfully looked for common ground, but he too declined to join in anything I organised which did not change matters greatly as in eleven years I had only once or twice seen him at Chapter or Synod. The seven senior men of St Helen's were more formidable. To meet them in their vestry, for moral support I took with me my deacon Georgie Heskins who was heavily pregnant and some extracts on relevant Bible passages from John Boswell's book *Homosexuality in Western Christian Tradition*. which meant we played textual table tennis for about an hour. The men were courteous but formal and at the end Sir Timothy Hoare asked how homosexuals see Evangelicals. I suggested it was like a black man looking at the Dutch Reformed Church in South Africa. 'Ouch' he replied.

By now – 1986 – AIDS was beginning to rear its ugliness in England – I had taken my first AIDS funeral two years before, so I travelled to the States early in the year to meet hospital chaplains and others working in the field to learn what we Christians should be doing and on my return I called together clergy in London who were concerned. We formed 'The Ministers Group' and over the next five years organised Services of Healing and Conferences. To begin with we arranged for a conference at King's College London in April 1986, which was set up by Georgie Heskins and John Holden (who had taken over as Priest/Counsellor from John Lee in 1984). John had worked with deaf people, had been helping at All Saints Margaret Street and is a gentle priest who did his professional training whilst he was with us and is now a full time therapist. The Conference at King's was attended by a large number of clergy and laity who probably for the first time heard about the horrors of HIV from Bishop Richard Holloway, Prof Michael Adler of the Middlesex Hospital and Geraldine Mulready of St Mary's Hospital. At the end of the day the Bishop said his vocabulary had been widened by all he had heard. 'Up until now I had thought rimming and frottage were West Country solicitors.'

In September 1986 the London Bishops' Staff Meeting asked me to spend an hour with them discussing our response to the HIV virus, so given the shortness of time I focused particularly on the needs of clergy and told them that given the number of homosexual clergy in the Diocese it was likely that ten or more would be affected in the next few years. One of the bishops agreed to discuss early retirement and pensions with the Church Commissioners and the following year one of the clergy I was caring for was helped enormously. His bishop, Mark Santer of Kensington, showed great compassion and care because on the day he was appointed to the See of Birmingham he spent most of the day comforting the man's father and was very supportive of the bewildered congregation at the funeral. The bishops also agreed to discuss guidelines for consulting church wardens; dealing with the media etc. These guidelines were given to Area Deans but I believe all clergy now need to know what happens if they develop symptoms of AIDS as at present there is a temptation to secrecy and cover up.

In November the Ministers Group organised a Service of Healing in St Botolph's at which Fr Michael Lopes, a Dominican from San Francisco preached powerfully. 200 were present and we asked everyone in the congregation to come forward for the laying on of hands. The following April we invited Bishop Swing of California to visit England and share his experience of AIDS ministry with us. He gave a very moving address at the Healing Service in Marylebone Parish Church and I also arranged for him to have an hour's confidential meeting with the Bishops of the London and Southwark dioceses. He told me that when he went to California Diocese some years earlier he had no experience whatever of the gay world and had not known of AIDS, but over the years his experience of the terrible suffering of so many had changed his somewhat homophobic Virginian views and I knew that his clergy and people held him in the very highest regard. With his wife he stayed with us at Tredegar Square where we laid in a store of Jack Daniels whisky to help the radio interviews. He agreed to visit the London Bishops' staff meeting on condition that the Bishop's chauffeur, Fred, should drive him to a golf course in the afternoon. He was a very refreshing, inspiring man to have around.

In November 1987 the General Synod debated a Report by the Board for Social Responsibility on AIDS. The Bishop of Gloucester, John Yates, introducing the session said AIDS is 'a threat to health and life which crosses all frontiers and spares nobody.' The proceedings were mercifully free of the 'God's Judgement' type of speeches and the Bishop stressed that the primary need 'is to show the face of love and compassion.' He called the Church to emphasise that adherence to the traditional teaching on chastity and fidelity would halt the spread of AIDS through sexual intercourse, 'This should be done positively and attractively rather than negatively and judgementally.' In my speech I said I was grateful that people were not taking their prejudices for a walk and suggested that action was needed at parish level as had been done in the Hackney Deanery, where, under the leadership of Evan Jones the Area Dean the subject had been studied, the Health Authority and local councillors had been lobbied and a network of carers had been set up. I asked that the Church appoint a full time adviser following the example of the United Reformed Church in England. Five years later this still had not been done so St Botolph's appointed a full time minister, Brother Colin Wilfed SSF, to care for those affected by the virus. St Botolph's also opened a hostel for three people in 1989. The Church Urban Fund and Crusaid fortunately gave financial help to this project.

I am often asked why we should make a special case of AIDS. Do not all terminal illnesses merit our compassion? Indeed, and I hope Christians are involved in caring for those afflicted but in the AIDS field we have to remember that sufferers have nearly all the taboos of our society heaped upon them – death, drugs, disfigurement, bereavement, sexually transmitted disease and belonging to sexual minority groups. The list is horrendous and I have no doubt Christ stands side by side with those affected. Over the years I have been astounded at the love and compassion shown by the gay community and by the outstanding courage shown by those living with the virus. With Rabbi Lionel Blue I have helped arrange four conferences for people affected and at the end of each I come away with my faith strengthened and my spirit lifted. We in this country now realise AIDS is not a gay plague nor a punishment for sins. (If it were so I would have expected Hitler to have at least had herpes.) It is the most horrendous disease which challenges us in the churches to surround it with all the compassion we can muster.

11 ALL MY FACULTIES

'Much evil has flowed from the fact that the Rector failed to get a Faculty.'

George Newsome, Chancellor of the Diocese of London

During my Californian holiday in September, 1987 I was almost thrown out of bed one night by an earthquake. Then, returning to England my car was demolished by a falling tree when the hurricane, with bursts of 94 mph winds hit London on the night of 15 October. These were as nothing compared to the storms of the next seven months surrounding St Botolph's.

Tony Higton, Rector of Hawkwell, Essex and a prominent Evangelical, described by the journalist, Andrew Brown as 'the Church of England's self appointed scourge of heretics, Hindus and homosexuals', had tabled a Private Member's motion to be discussed at the November General Synod which said that sexual intercourse should only take place between men and women within marriage; that 'fornication, adultery and homosexual acts are sinful in all circumstances' and asked that Christian leaders should be exemplary in all spheres of morality including sexual morality 'as a condition of being appointed to or remaining in office'. 167 out of the 550 members had signed the Motion and it was rumoured that Mrs Thatcher personally approved it. I had put in a wrecking amendment which asked Synod to affirm the essentials of the Biblical message that human love is a reflection of divine love; that all relationships should therefore be characterised by permanency and commitment. I also asked for the education of young people and parents in the dangers spiritual and physical of sexual promiscuity whether heterosexual or homosexual.

During the month before Synod there was some media coverage but I only agreed to be interviewed once with Mr Higton on Radio 4. In the discussion I said I regretted that Christians seem obsessed by what goes on below the belt instead of looking at whole relationships and told the interviewer that I thought the Motion was a grave and gross insult to the gay community who had already been so badly treated by the Church. She seemed to agree. The same week at the launch of his pamphlet *Sexuality and the Church* Mr Higton once again referred to the pornographic literature he had seen on sale at St Botolph's and the next day several seedy members of the dirty raincoat brigade visited the Church to see what they could find. They were disappointed because even the four LGCM pamphlets usually on sale at the church bookstall had mysteriously been removed. In reply to the many reports in the press I put out a press release which said the Parochial Church Council welcomed LGCM's presence in the tower of the church as it was a symbol and sign that they are members of the Christian Family. Only *The Times* printed it but our own poetess and full time crypt volunteer the doughty Doris Boyd penned:

> Mr Bigton puff and power
> Paid a visit to our Tower
> After listening to his crap
> We've become a tourist trap
> Lots of people visit us
> Just take the tube
> or come by Bus

In fact we had already been attacked for selling so-called pornographic literature at the time of the Queen's visit seven years earlier and also a few months before Synod when Diana Core visited the LGCM office without revealing her membership of Childwatch and then went to Bishopsgate Police station to make a complaint about what she had seen. Geoffrey Dickens, the Tory MP for Littleborough and Saddleworth told *The Evening Standard*, (30.4.87) 'We found it to be absolutely full of explicit literature on gay and lesbian love and paedophilia. Members of the Childwatch team felt 'physically ill' after their visit he said. According to the *Standard*, Mr Dickens felt that anyone known to be homosexual should not be ordained in the Church of England – too many homosexual priests would be simply incapable of keeping their hands off the choir boys. Valentine Law the *Standard* reporter called by appointment and was shown up the tiny tower staircase to the LGCM office where the offending books were said to be on sale, the most lurid of all he felt was *The Joy of Gay Sex* published by Mitchell Beazley. Mr Valentine wrote 'Inside the Office, Mr Kirker pointed at the posters of naked men on the wall. He said with some justification, "they are hardly lurid photos, they are part of the safe sex campaign. You'll find them in health centres, hospitals, gay centres and pubs. There is nothing untoward about our being involved in promoting these issues." ' The Terrence Higgins Trust posters advocating safe sex were in fact of men stripped to the waist, not fully naked.

It is important to say that the church bookstall on public view just inside the main door usually but not always contained three or four LGCM pamphlets on spirituality and gay sexuality. The books referred to by Mr

Dickens and others were in the tower office – admission to which was usually by appointment only. Somewhat reluctantly Richard Kirker, full time secretary of LGCM, had already agreed to stop selling *The Joy of Gay Sex* and to withdraw the Terrence Higgins Trust safe sex leaflets which need to be explicit to get their message across to sexually active males and thus, I hope, save lives. Explicit language and drawings are necessary to draw attention to deadly practices; I also firmly rejected criticism of *Sexual Experience between Men and Boys* being sold from the church. It is a highly regarded, serious academic study of pederasty by Parker Rossman, a professor at Yale, which certainly did not condone sex with minors as was falsely alleged. In my own counselling work with people attracted to young children and teenagers I have always found it difficult to gain knowledge and insights into their condition so this book filled a real need.

On the morning of the General Synod debate, 11 November I felt anxious but calm despite all the media attention. Mr Higton's opening speech was a thinly veiled attack on homosexuals which largely ignored the fornication and adultery mentioned in the motion. In his ponderous way he listed all the promiscuous horrors he had heard were being perpetrated by the homosexual clergy and laity.

It was my impression that most Synod members were unhappy at the shallowness of it all and embarrassed that we had been catapulted into a serious debate on sexuality listened in to by the nation at large despite the fact that we had been given no Report on the subject by the Bishops, their theological advisors or the Board of Social Responsibility. I was called to speak fairly early in the debate and here is what I said:

'This motion seems to me to be a sort of moral M1, an open road, a motorway, down which we are being invited to drive at speed, recklessly knocking down everyone in the way and particularly those who are most vulnerable in our society. So we hit the single parent with condemnation and calumny; we injure the divorced; we maim the remarried, for in biblical terms they are adulterers. Many in this Synod and beyond have fought hard to recognise second marriages – how can we now say that adultery is sinful in all circumstances? Then finally we knock homosexuals into the gutter, for that is, I believe, the hidden agenda of this motion, once again to heap abuse on a minority group who in my view have suffered enough at the Church's hands. This motion is a negative piece of work, lacking in faith, lacking in hope and lacking in love.

It is negative because it does not speak to the real world; it addresses only the first-time married and the promiscuous, and in the middle are many people seeking guidance. I believe that my amendment gives it. It is negative because it is aimed solely at those who fully accept the

Christian ideal, so it can hardly be said to be for 'the well-being of society' since the majority are not committed Christian believers. It is negative because it refuses to face facts and denies the splendid variety of God's creation. Leaving aside all those who are branded as so-called adulterers and fornicators, it is a fact that approximately four per cent of our population, a larger number than the ethnic minorities, are exclusively or predominently homosexual, about two and a half million people in the United Kingdom – far too large a number to be the result of a deficient upbringing or learned behaviour – and the vast majority of these people are not called to celibacy nor are they capable of it.

Why can we not accept the fact that homosexuals will by their nature, want to form same-sex relationships and will need positive guidance from us as they do so? I believe that my amendment offers that guidance, with its encouragement of stability, commitment and permanence in all relationships. Today we are faced, as we well know, with the scourge of AIDS, which demands a positive, helpful response from Christians. This motion obviously wants to combat promiscuity but, as it denies good, stable relationships, it will have the opposite effect. It is no good saying that homosexuals are promiscuous; we must ask why they are promiscuous and if they have been given negative advice for two thousand years they have had no guidelines except 'Stop it'.

Why are we frightened of opening our eyes to see the splendid variety of God's creation? He has made us black, brown, white, male, female, heterosexual, homosexual, tall, short, fat, thin, Thatchers, Kinnocks, Holloways, Brindleys. Blessed be God! When I was in America recently I went to see the film Maurice. It describes the tentative progress of a gay man towards self-realisation in Edwardian England, and so you can imagine the pain. The one line that had the American audience rocking with laughter and applauding – I gather the same is true in London – was EM Forster's immortal phrase, 'The English have always been disinclined to accept human nature'.

In all the literature supporting this motion, I detect a strong smell of cowardice because it attacks, and has encouraged the media to attack, the gay clergy who cannot defend themselves. Many of them are ministering effectively in inner city areas and they owe their stability to deep, good relationships. Because of their public office, they cannot reply to the insults which are heaped on them. This attack has already started in the gutter press, and I hope that the proposers of this motion realise their responsibility for it.

Why then vote for this amendment of mine? Simply because it speaks positively to our Church and to our nation. It seeks to stop the damage done to homosexuals over the centuries by encouraging them to lead good, godly, lives and to form good, godly permanent relationships. I have counselled gay people for the past 20 years, and I have seen the suffering and the hurt and the oppression that we have caused. A short time ago I had to conduct the funeral of a man who had been with his lover for 27 years. Should I have faced his partner at the crematorium and told him that we judge his friendship by his genital acts? Should I have told him that he has sinned for 27 years, that his love 'falls short' and that he needs forgiveness? This motion says nothing to that man or to others like him. I thank God that such deep relationships are becoming more common, whether we like it or not.

I agree with *The Church Times* which said recently that this motion 'expresses a part of the mind of the Church, because many are remembering Our Lord's words about throwing stones and at the same time realising that the denunciations of arsenokoitai in the Bible seem to refer to perverts who are by nature heterosexual and by habit promiscuous'. *The Church Times* asks, 'Does the new understanding of the homosexual condition sometimes call for new ethics or at least for agnosticism about guilt?' to which I reply, 'Yes.' Do we not believe that the Holy Spirit can lead us into new truths?

I do not understand why we cannot agree to disagree on this issue as we do on many others. Some priests marry divorced people in church, some do not. Some Christians agree with the ordination of women, some do not. Some support the Gloucester report in saying that there are circumstances in which a homosexual relationship can be accepted, some do not. Can we not in this time of transition agree to disagree?

I began by talking about the M1. When I was in Los Angeles recently people in traffic jams were shooting at each other on the freeways. Needless to say, I drove with Anglican restraint and courtesy. Why do we need to shoot at each other by proposing motions like this? Can we not listen to each other, pray, debate and learn? The bishops have appointed a working party to assist that process. Why should we now, by passing this motion or the Bishops' amendment, tie their hands, telling them what conclusion we expect them to come to?

Finally – and in this I agree with The Bishop of London – part (iii) of the motion suggests that ministers may only be appointed or remain in office if they lead exemplary lives. Well, as Canon Rhymes has remarked – I do not know who would be left. There are seven deadly sins, not just one: lust, pride, sloth, gluttony, covetousness, envy, anger. If we have to leave after committing these, the Church will be very short-staffed indeed.

I regret the tone of this motion. We simply must not send this sort of message to the nation, for the reasons that I have given. All relationships are fragile today. Most people are struggling to love in difficult, painful circumstances. They need encouragement, not condemnation."

My amendment was lost 46-325 with possibly 50 or so abstentions. Those voting for it had to hold their hands high to be counted so I was able to see that my supporters were mainly women accompanied by a handful of gay people. Several gay men either voted against or absented themselves from the Chamber. The Synod passed a Motion drawn up by the House of Bishops which removed homosexual acts from the company of fornication and adultery and thus slightly weakened Higton's proposal. It affirmed the Biblical and traditional teaching on chastity and fidelity in personal relationships and said sexual intercourse is an act of total commitment which belongs properly within a permanent married relationship. It also said that fornication and adultery which are sins against this ideal should be met with penitence and compassion and it stated homosexual genital acts fall short of the ideal of a permanent married relationship. Voting was 388-19. I was one of the nineteen. The following morning I received a telephone message from two gay friends who have lived together for many years saying 'Tell Malcolm we are going away for the weekend to fall short.'

The next day, Bernard Levin writing in *The Times* said he had been overwhelmed by listening 'to an array of ordained clergymen chatting happily and knowledgeably about perversion and intercourse, condoms, genitals and and masturbation.' He said I had led the attack in 'a most exemplary demonstration of what Christian Charity entails.' The tabloids were not so kind with headlines screaming 'Pulpit poofs can stay', 'Holy Homos Escape Ban' and 'Church votes to keep Gay Vicars'. I gave only two interviews – to Laurence Spicer of LBC and (with Mr Higton) to Claire Rayner on the Jimmy Young Show. Douglas Rhymes the distinguished retired Canon of Southwark Cathedral was immensely brave in talking about his own homosexuality on BBC TV Newsnight programme and millions must have been surprised by his integrity and honesty. I certainly depended a lot on his support. It was about this time that an ex priest, Alan Saunders, accompanied by someone who he said needed counselling but who turned out to be a reporter with a hidden tape recorder, went round various gay clergy and got them to talk about their sex lives. Soon after the typescripts appeared in *The People*. If most people had the honesty and courage of Douglas this would not happen.

I had a mountain of mail 12-1 in favour of what I'd said in Synod and I particularly appreciated Donald Reeves, Rector of St James Piccadilly telling me 'you have consistently been on the side of the underdog. That is real gospel stuff!' A retired Canon in Cheltenham wrote to ask how I could condone buggery and bestiality and another retired priest told me, 'you appear to be over-preoccupied with sex which is not becoming in a priest. If my wife and I were a youngish married couple in your parish our reaction would be to keep away from you.'

At a buffet supper party held on the evening of the debate the new Archdeacon of London, George Cassidy suggested I should offer my resignation as Area Dean to the Bishop, whom he thought would refuse it. I could not understand why George Cassidy said this as I had done nothing wrong. It was the second warning bell to sound about him and his views. Shortly before the debate, on 5 November he told me Bishop Graham had said to him 'Malcolm will worry me into an early grave.' As the Bishop was on sick leave I was greatly distressed and wrote at once to Bishop Graham saying I had no alternative but to stand up to the likes of Higton. I received no reply. When later, at a clergy Conference in All Saints London Colney, I asked the Bishop about his remark he brushed it aside saying George was exaggerating.

Two weeks later I received a note from the Diocesan Registrar, David Faull, asking that I petition for a Faculty to rent LGCM the tower room. I later learnt that the Chancellor of the Diocese, George Newsome had himself read the Report of the Synod Debate and had realised LGCM were trespassing as he put it. David Faull told me the present Lord Mayor would enter an objection and I must hurry things along.

A Faculty is a written document issued by the Chancellor or Judge of a Diocese giving permission for a proposed change in the fabric of a church. Usually it has to be granted if someone wants to repair or restore any part of the building or its contents, or parishioners wish to install something new like a statue or showcase. The Chancellor asks the Diocesan Advisory Committee to give evidence concerning the artistic merits or suitability of what is proposed and those who object are invited to say why. The Chancellor then makes a decision. If the matter is contentious then he will hear the arguments in what is called a Consistory Court. I had not realised until the previous January that a Faculty is needed to rent a room in a Church. The Bishop and Archdeacon obviously knew LGCM were renting a room but no objection had been raised by them in eleven years.

My PCC had realised in the previous January that we should have obtained a Faculty so I had asked Faull to prepare the necessary lease for LGCM to sign. He had delegated the task to one of his assistants, Paul Morris. When they sent me the draft lease in April neither of them had suggested the matter would be difficult or controversial. Why had these legal experts not warned me what might happen? I think they both must shoulder a large slice of the blame for all the suffering caused to so many over the next six months. At that time we had no Archdeacon as Frank Harvey 'The thug who says his Prayers' (his own description) had died the previous autumn. We all regretted the passing of this tough, honest and caring man, and wondered who would succeed him? The Bishop had asked me to stay behind after a Diocesan meeting on 6 April and said he regretted he could not make me Archdeacon because of my stance on certain matters. 'It might be possible elsewhere but not here.'

I felt very bruised by the Synod Debate but I was heartened two weeks later by an invitation to lunch at Lambeth Palace. The Archbishop, Robert Runcie, had been my Principal at Cuddesdon Theological College and we talked over why homosexuality had hardly been mentioned during my time there. Now, together with the ordination of women to the priesthood, it had a high profile. He is well known for his evenly balanced statements – on the one hand, on the other hand – so I could not draw him to say anything definite but at least he listened to myself, Jim Cotter, the priest writer and Jeremy Younger, then a curate at Bow, who made some forceful statements. As we left I told him the meeting was a giant step forward as I could not imagine Fisher or Coggan entertaining us.

I now had to get myself and the PCC a good lawyer as the Registrar who had been acting for us would be acting for the Archdeacon. I phoned Garth Moore, City Rector and Chancellor of several dioceses, who had given me sound advice in the past and he suggested John Underwood who had been a friend of mine and of his for many years. John came to St Botolph's on 2 December and I explained to him that LGCM had been in residence for 11 years, and that the PCC in the previous January had decided they should stay although there was some feeling in LGCM that they might perhaps want to leave after twelve months. St Botolph's staff who met regularly with Richard Kirker had decided, despite the fact we needed the tower room for our homeless work, that they wanted LGCM to remain. The PCC had approved a tenancy agreement and sent it in April 1987 to their committee but nothing had been heard since. Archdeacon Cassidy, a committed Evangelical, would be no friend of ours and anyway the Chancellor wanted a quick decision. Should I petition for a Faculty? John, to whom St Botolph's owes a huge debt for his wise counsel and support, suggested I try to resolve things without a confrontation. Had the Archdeacon been Frank Harvey this would have been possible because we would have had several pints of beer together and I would have quietly arranged LGCM's departure after a decent interval. I knew that their members considered the room less than ideal because it could only be reached up a long, steep spiral staircase and every time the church bells were rung the walls and floor moved around and the noise was deafening. It was also difficult if not impossible to welcome casual callers many of whom came from overseas. If the Church Authorities were heavy handed however, there would be no chance of a reconciliation. John promised to approach the Bishop, but Graham refused to speak with him. Archdeacon Cassidy told me to apply for a Faculty by 15 December or he would apply himself for a Faculty to remove LGCM.

On Wednesday 9 December – two days before the PCC would decide what to do – I left a message with George's secretary asking to talk matters over. Despite several more calls he did not contact me until Friday at 4 pm It soon became apparent from his telephone conversation that he wanted the matter to come to court, that he felt the Press would not be interested and that he did not consider LGCM to be a Christian organisation. Four times I begged him to see what damage a court case would do. In the heat of the moment I said 'If you want a fight I'll give it to you.' Almost immediately I regretted this, particularly as George told people I had threatened him. I later apologised to him.

The PCC on 11th, listened to what had happened and asked me to negotiate. The Archdeacon had finished the conversation by agreeing to speak to the Bishop and Registrar to see if an agreement could be reached without a Hearing. So we all had high hopes. However, the PCC felt that if this failed I, not the Archdeacon, must apply to the Chancellor on 15th. On the Monday morning I delivered a letter by hand to George asking that I be given time to resolve the matter pastorally. 'I do not mistake the urgency, I am not prevaricating. A court case would curry lurid publicity and incidentally damage our work with the homeless.' I received no reply and when I telephoned on 15th the secretary said the Archdeacon was not available and had said 'there was nothing to add to what he had already said.' I therefore was forced much against my will to apply for a Faculty.

The PCC meeting on Sunday 20 December was the best I ever attended. John Underwood passed me a note. 'You are wonderfully blessed by a PCC of extraordinary quality.' They decided to continue their support for LGCM by 11 votes to 5, with three abstentions.

On 6 January 1988 the new Dean of St Paul's, Eric Evans, was asked at a press conference if he knew LGCM had an office in the City. The Archdeacon, who was present, said he knew and was taking steps to remove them. The next morning most of the papers reported this on front or back pages and I was woken at 7.20 am for a statement. Later in front of the television cameras I read my statement which said that we believed the presence of LGCM's office in a consecrated building was a powerful sign that homosexuals are welcome in the Church. 'It gives them an opportunity to consider how they might put their theology and their sexuality together'. I stressed we certainly did not agree with all the statements of the organisation or its secretary. Reporters visited St Botolph's all day and one got into the crypt centre and asked if the young homeless men there were at risk from the users of the tower office. The press gave us a responsible write up the next day and Barry O'Brien of *The Daily Telegraph*, somewhat surprisingly for that paper, put our case extremely well. The Archdeacon was quoted as saying that one of the reasons he wanted the Movement expelled was that they gained credibility by being in a church building. That afternoon I went to see Brian Masters, Bishop of Edmonton, to ask him to mediate on our behalf but he said there was nothing he could do. Sadly it seemed the battle was on, troops were already in trenches and firing at each other from prepared positions.

The PCC at its meeting on 10th January asked that a public relations Officer advise us and fortunately Lawrence Spicer agreed to help particularly in our relationships with the media. At the London Area Bishops Council five days later a member asked what was happening. I said I was appalled at the prospect of a court case which might damage everyone and I was angry that there had been no opportunity to discuss a strategy to avoid confrontation. The Bishop berated me for five minutes and said I should realise how much he had defended me over the years. He did not of course answer my remarks, and afterwards once again said he had had a complaint about St Botolph's sending gay literature to a woman. I asked him to provide proof and heard nothing more. George Cassidy said lawyer must now speak to lawyer and I should realise Consistory Courts were part of the life of an Archdeacon.

Many people were surprised when they learnt of LGCM's presence in St Botolph's. Little publicity had surrounded their eleven years and all mail had been sent to a box number. One of our volunteers, a monk, wrote to the Archdeacon saying he had regularly visited the church for four years and could still not find the notorious bookstall or office. He agreed the existence of LGCM was a sin but a sin resulting primarily from the church isolating, marginalising and persecuting homosexuals.

During the next three months I spent a great deal of time explaining and defending our stance. I was surprised at the hundreds of letters of support which arrived and the affirmation I received from my fellow City clergy. Nearly all the Chapter felt I had been badly treated and were shocked when the Archdeacon twice refused to come and discuss the matter with them. One member told me he disagreed with my views on homosexuality but was impressed by the quality of pastoral care we offered. 'Someone has to care for them and I trust your pastoral judgment.' To others it was a learning experience as for the first time they realised the hurt, rejection and persecution homosexuals face almost daily. Another told me how he had decided to remonstrate with a best man who in a wedding speech in front of an elderly bride groom had said, 'I was beginning to think you were bent.'

A few of our supporting parishes wrote to say they could no longer help us. A church in Swindon who had supported us for a while was confronted by a very wealthy member of its congregation who threatened to withdraw his large covenant if the church continued helping us. The churchwardens were dispatched to interview me with a tape recorder so I carefully told my side of the story. The vicar later telephoned to tell me that the Parochial Church Council had agreed to give in to what I thought amounted to blackmail. I told him that I thought the man might well use the same trick again to get his way. Interestingly enough the curate wrote to tell me that he would no longer support his church financially but send us a donation instead. A few individuals including two millionaires wrote to withdraw their covenants. One has since asked me to lunch and apologised most graciously for what he had done.

On the other hand several new supporters arrived and donations to our legal costs came from all and sundry including Coventry Cathedral and several parishes. A lawyer wrote offering a very large sum from his Trust.

The London Diocesan Council for Christian Jewish Understanding had met at St Botolph's since George Appleton started it in the 1960s. In January one of its members proposed it should move because it might be damaged by association with us. Fortunately the other members out-voted her.

At the end of March I was standing in our Administrator's office when I felt shooting pains across my chest and had difficulty in breathing. I collapsed on to the floor and lost consciousness momentarily. Jude supported my head and held my hand whilst Richard Basch phoned for an ambulance. Unfortunately there was a queue of calls and by the time the girl phoned back I was sitting in a chair feeling decidedly unwell. I was taken to hospital by car where I had all sorts of tests. The doctors told me my heart was OK and asked if I had been under any stress lately? The body obviously needed a rest so I was told to go home and stay there for a fortnight which I did. It meant I missed Holy Week and Easter, which was a great sadness to me.

I did, however, go with our lawyer a week later to see our barrister, Timothy Bryden to get his opinion about the case. I also saw the Bishop who stressed we needed a negotiated settlement but did little to obtain it.

He referred briefly to his March Newsletter which had begun 'I had hoped to continue my series on the Ten Commandments but I must refer to the matter of St Botolph's Aldgate.' I complained of several inaccuracies in his account and later it was agreed that I could reply in his April letter, which I did. I also could not resist asking him why at his own Bishop's Conference for clergy and laity on 19 March, the Bishop of Fulham, John Klyberg was not present, Archdeacon Cassidy was at Twickenham to see a rugger match and the bishop himself left after twenty minutes saying he had a heavy cold. Was it because the subject of the day's conference was 'Sexuality'? Well over a year before the Bishop had asked me and a doctor to organise this conference and he had agreed to us inviting two speakers – Dr Jack Dominian, the famous Roman Catholic writer and Liz Sheddon, Director of Lay Training for the Diocese. Were the hierachy scared that the dreaded subject of homosexuality would raise its head? My co-organiser, looking rather pale withdrew two weeks beforehand, but all their fears were unfounded as homosexuality was only mentioned briefly in the afternoon question session, although later I was suprised to hear that Dr Leonard had sent for the priest who asked the question and remonstrated with him. I chaired the conference and felt it to be a great success. One hundred and fifty people were present, the atmosphere was relaxed and thoughtful and certainly did not reflect the fears of the hierarchy. I, of course, received no thanks for the enormous amount of effort I had put into the organisation of the event.

The opinion given to St Botolph's by the barrister, Mr Bryden, was clear. We had no chance whatever of being granted a Faculty as LGCM was a controversial organisation and no controversial organisation could be allowed to lease space in a consecrated building. He pointed out that Chancellor George Newsome, by then 78 years old and not known for his liberal views, had already intimated to our lawyer that we would not succeed, as had two other senior Chancellors. The decision whether or not to permit the occupation of a room is entirely the matter for the discretion of the Chancellor who must satisfy himself that the use of the room will be 'suitable'. Counsel confirmed what I had begun to suspect and after debate the PCC took his advice to withdraw their application. This was not as easy as it sounds as the Chancellor has to give permission for withdrawal and this must be done in his Court. I now had to persuade LGCM that this was the best course of action for them and us. They were conjoined with St Botolph's on the application for a Faculty so if we withdrew they would be left on their own. I realised that they wanted an opportunity to prove that they were a bone fide Christian organisation and that the Archdeacon's allegations were false. Despite 'flu I travelled to Southampton to speak to their Annual General Meeting and Canon Eric Jarvis, a City incumbent representing the Chapter also came, to advise withdrawal. The costs of proceeding to a full Hearing would be astronomic, probably as much as £80,000. Several other parishes in the London Area who were having difficulties with the Archdeacon were also facing huge legal bills and like us pondering on the morality of it all. Clergy and laity from five large parishes in the Archdeacon's Area had already been meeting regularly to see what could be done. The Bishop was later to meet with them and ignore their demands.

On 25 April, John Underwood applied to have the Hearing adjourned to give us time to deal with the matter with proper Christian care but this was refused, so on 11 May, at an all day Hearing in Westminster, I was given permission to withdraw the Faculty. 'The Rector', said the Chancellor, 'must throw himself on the mercy of the Court'. It was such a good line I wrote it down immediately. During the proceedings, a mixture of Toytown and Trollope, I was humiliated and told 'much evil has flowed' from my actions. I suggested to the Chancellor that as his was a Christian Court it should be concerned with the pastoral responsibilities I have for members of LGCM but he was not impressed. In agreeing to St Botolph's request to withdraw he ordered that the PCC should pay the Archdeacon's costs and that I should institute eviction proceedings to remove the organisation by 30 September. I was forbidden to speak about the case and I told *The Church Times* that this was just as well as my views were unprintable. We later learned that star witnesses for the prosecution would have included a former Lord Mayor and our old pal the Revd Tony Higton.

The night before the LGCM's annual meeting they received the substance of George Cassidy's case against them. This has never been published but alleges that the Movement condoned breaking the law; stocked obscene literature and distributed it, again contravening the law.

The Guildhall court had been booked for four days so that the Chancellor could hear the application for a Faculty. I had been telephoned every week by *The Yorkshire Post* asking when this would be as they wanted a reporter to come to London to witness the fireworks. The Court was in fact packed with press and public and Mr Higton sat with the two QCs representing the Archdeacon. LGCM was represented by an able young solicitor, Jane Hickman who was not an ecclesiastical lawyer but learnt her brief quickly. Several of her profession who are adept in walking through the minefield of Church Law had refused the brief presumably because it might offend their other ecclesiastical clients. This absence of willing ecclesiastical lawyers prepared to defend LGCM caused grave concern and led to a discussion whether the Movement would be in a position to defend itself.

LGCM's QC, who was known as the Rolls Royce of legal procedural detail, argued that the Movement should never have been part of the application in the first place. The Chancellor seemed impressed by the arguments and after several hours agreed. There was no mention of withdrawal by LGCM and he said the Archdeacon could ask for costs but it was unclear who would pay them. In the event LGCM only paid their own costs of £8,000.

The next morning the tabloids again screamed abuse – 'Church Poofters Quit HQ' said *The Sun* but several papers expressed disquiet. *The Independent* in a leader, 18 May, ' A Scandal to the Faithful' asked why the Archdeacon had not heeded the words of St Paul, 'The very fact you have law suits among you means that you have been completely defeated already.' The writer said 'The whole process looks like simple, vindictive bullying. Outsiders can only conclude that the opponents of the Movement were not content to drive it from St Botolph's but wanted those associated with its stay to be publicly humiliated and landed with heavy personal costs. That also is a scandal for the Church'.

Father Kenneth Leech, theologian and Director of the Runnymede Trust returned his licence to officiate in the London Diocese saying St Botolph's was a target of attack and calumny 'by some of the most unpleasant people I have ever encountered in the Christian Church or anywhere else'. Victor Stock, Rector of St Mary-le-Bow, in a letter to *The Independent* said that many City clergy were 'distressed at the whole tenor of the conduct of this case especially as we have written as a clergy chapter on two occasions asking the Archdeacon to meet us as the City clergy without avail. Those of us with experience of Consistory courts know all too well that there are no winners.'

On 29 May several diocesan clergy, most of whom had no links with LGCM wrote to the Bishop of London deploring the way things had been handled and saying the resort to law was an inappropriate response to a pastoral problem. Gay people, particularly in the current hostile climate, should be listened to with respect and love. They said each party should pay their own costs, and privately to me many of them intimated that if I was forced to pay the Archdeacon's costs then they would send me the money their parishes should pay to the Diocesan Common Fund.

In the event St Botolph's were not asked to pay the Archdeacon's costs which amounted to approximately £20,000. Our own fees which amounted to £6,468 were paid by friends and supporters who included two Trusts, several congregations and many individuals. Coventry Cathedral sent £500. The Provost, John Petty, told me he had preached a sermon on Reconciliation in the City, had mentioned the Archbishop's Commission on Urban Priority Areas, then spoke about the problems facing St Botolph's.

He asked for gifts and cash poured in including a donation from a church for the deaf via their minister, Marion Fry.

On 9 June I kept the 25th anniversary of my priesting and four hundred people came to St Botolph's for a magnificent Service and reception which was a great affirmation for me. The Bishop of Lincoln, Robert Hardy preached and blessed our new Chapel of Peace and presents poured in including an Edward Seago watercolour from the congregation and a Rowlands Prichard painting from LGCM. My old friends the choir of St Barnabas Woodford conducted by Ray Chandler provided the music which included 'I Was Glad' by Hubert Parry. That evening I was very relaxed and happy especially when a spoof message arrived 'Best wishes on your retirement, from George Cassidy!' The following week it was reported to me that a Bishop's staff meeting of another diocese in the metropolitan area were discussing who could advise them about purchasing a new computer. 'Why not the Archdeacon of London?' suggested a Canon. 'He's not user friendly' said the Diocesan Bishop.

Things returned to normal but on 10 July, *The Mail on Sunday* carried a three page article 'Scandal of Gay Clergy' in which it suggested certain City churches were 'open pick-up joints'. It was quite obvious that the reporter, Iain Walker, had got most of his information from the Archdeacon, whose photograph took up a third of a page. It repeated the allegations of pornography being sold at St Botolph's, pictured the safe sex pamphlet of the Terrence Higgins Trust in a provocative public manner and it detailed some of the case which George had prepared for the Court Hearing. I had been told by the Chancellor to keep quiet but here was the Archdeacon rehearsing all his arguments again, so at the Area Dean's meeting at London House two days later I asked the Bishop of London to reprimand his Archdeacon for giving the interview. Graham said, 'It is a matter between George, you and I, not for this meeting'. I protested most strongly but the Bishop got very angry and asked if I realised how much stress the Archdeacon had been under and I should remember that he had no way to reply to allegations. I suggested he might have spoken to the City Deanery Chapter, not the gutter press. Once again after a great number of words the Bishop had not replied to my arguments.

A somewhat similar scene took place in the Area Deans' meeting at London House the following October when I asked Bishop Leonard why he had thrown out the St Hilda's Community, which included many people in favour of the Ordination of women, from St Benet's Chaplaincy, Queen Mary College in East London. 'I had to exert my authority,' he said, 'Once you start giving in who knows where it will lead.' I then asked if he realised that many now thought the Rule of Law had replaced the Rule of

Love in the London Diocese. He became very angry indeed and stormed out of the meeting saying 'You have only got me for two more years.'

By a strange coincidence on the very same day Tory MP John Marshall asked in the House of Commons how much the Church Commissioners paid each year to St Botolph's. He was told to consult the London Diocese so I wrote and asked the reason for his question. His reply was evasive.

I was further humiliated by being forced by the Chancellor on 5 September 1988 to go to the Lord Mayor's and City of London Court to obtain an Eviction Order to meet the imposed dateline of LGCM's move. This was part of the Chancellor's instructions of the previous May. Fortunately no-one was present, except someone asleep in the back row. There was no need for the Order to be served as LGCM left the church on 10 September with a triumphant Service of Exodus at which Ken Leech preached. The Liturgy moved through the recognition of our oppression and the need for reconciliation; the telling of the story in prayer, dance and song, then the sharing of the Eucharistic meal – food for the journey. Then came the moving out of the church, the renewal of the Covenant and on the church steps the looking forward. 'It is our conviction that human sexuality in all its richness is a gift of God, gladly to be accepted, enjoyed and honoured, as a way of both expressing and growing in love in accordance with the life and teaching of Jesus Christ. Therefore it is our conviction that it is entirely compatible with the Christian faith not only to love another person of the same sex but also to express that love fully in a personal sexual relationship.' As I blessed the many people standing on the steps I looked across at Naomi Blake's statue dedicated to The Oppressed. The connection was clear.

The whole sad sorry affair was a disgrace to the Church and has done much damage to the way gays and lesbians regard Christianity. At the very time when homosexuals need acceptance and affirmation the Bishop, Chancellor and Archdeacon, used the rule of law to expel LGCM and slam the door in their face. May God forgive them. I find it hard to.

12 THREE SERMONS BY MALCOLM JOHNSON

On Hospitality

'When you have a party do not invite your friends, relations or rich neighbours, they will only ask you back again and so you will be repaid. When you give a party ask the poor the crippled, the lame, and so find happiness for they have no means of repaying you.'

Luke 16:10

No one seems to spell St Botolph's name correctly. I received letters addressed to the Rector of St Bolotovs (a Russian Saint?), St Bottle, St Botolophs and best of all St Buttocks. He is not exactly top of the Saintly Pops. Yet he did exist, living in a monastery near Leiston, Suffolk in the seventh century and was well known as a friendly Abbot who would give you a square meal or a bed for the night in accordance with the Benedictine Rule: 'Let all guests who arrive be received like Christ who will say I came as a guest and you received me'. The traveller on the doorstep is Christ Himself.

So you can forget St Christopher: he never existed. Botolph is the Patron Saint of hospitality, the travellers' saint, and that is why four of the churches by the City of London gates had him as their patron – Bishopsgate, Aldersgate, Aldgate and Billingsgate. All but the last remain today and are still places where travellers can call in and pray for strength to undertake their journey whether it be into the wilds of Essex via the Mile End Road or to the Board Room to make a decision affecting hundreds of people or to the Royal London Hospital to visit a friend. Churches, hospitals, hospices, hotels are places where we find refreshment, healing, rest and most of all hospitality – a very devalued word in our language. The German words Gastgeber- the guest giver, the one who gives to guests – and Gastfreundschaft – guest friendship or what is offered by hosts to guests, have greater meaning. What is hospitality? Fr Henri Nouwen says that to be hospitable is to convert a hostis, an enemy into a hospes, a guest, because hospitality is to create space where friendship can be expressed and nurtured and change can take place. I find that a very useful idea in our Crypt Centre where we offer physical space and many volunteers offer their time. 'Hospitality is not to change people but to offer them space where change can take place,' and this is not done in any Lady Bountiful way because for me it is a two way process of giving and receiving. One Christmas I discovered an eminent City gent carving the turkeys in the crypt kitchen. When I thanked him he said, 'Don't thank me Rector, I was divorced last year and my wife has taken the children. I was sitting at home feeling sorry for myself so I thought I'd come and give you a hand and I'm having a great time.'

Hospitality was an important Old Testament concept. Without it you would not have survived for long in the dry dusty Middle East of Our Lord's time. I see it, too, in modern America where because it was dangerous travelling around that huge country a hundred years ago a tradition of warm hospitality has grown up. It isn't long before you are offered a drink or meal and told to visit Uncle Fred in Florida should you go South.

Jesus was of course the perfect host, giving himself to everyone he met and much of his ministry took place around a table. Being an itinerant preacher he received hospitality and those who gave it experienced a blessing – think of Zaccheus opening up his home.

God is our Host here on earth. We are his guests and we have a responsibility to keep his house in good order and in our turn be good hosts to others. In reality we behave like teenagers who having been left to look after the family home proceed to abuse and neglect it and have to call the Yellow Pages to find a furniture restorer to repair the damage before our parents return.

You and I have 70 or 80 years, I hope, to live in God's home and accept his hospitality. How are you doing? The Church, the Community of believers, gets a lot of insults today but I think we should be proud that it was Christians who founded the schools, colleges and hospitals of our country to be places of hospitality and learning.

'When you have a party do not invite your friends, relations or rich neighbours, they will only ask you back again and so you will be repaid. When you give a party ask the poor, the crippled, the lame and so find happiness for they have no means of repaying you.' (Luke 16:10)

Be hospitable. We may not have the resources to found or fund a school or hospital but personally I'm proud that St Botolph's has opened four hostels for homeless women and men. It will be different for each congregation but the community that lives to itself dies to itself. The resources may be meagre but I am always surprised what is on offer in most parishes. A Church, a hall and a host of very talented people whose services have probably never been asked for – except to put money in a plate. Congregations are small so it is no use trying to solve all the worlds problems, – just choose, say two areas of suffering where it might be possible to do something given the resources you have. Each local area has different needs and it would be presumptuous of me to tell parishes what to do to be hospitable.

At Aldgate the answer was given to us in a dramatic way. George Appleton, the then Rector, found homeless people sitting and even sleeping in the churchyard. Nothing was being done for them so he filled the gap by opening up the crypt as a friendly hospitable place. Other parishes have other needs and other gaps to fill – the Hospice Movement is a good example of Christians being concerned about the lack of facilities for the terminally ill so people banded together to found hospices and what marvellous places they are of light, hope, joy and faith. It is important for us to work ecumenically if we are to have any effect.

There is another dimension to all this and it is summed up by the story of a priest who in the seventeenth century had to minister to hundreds of parishioners who were dying of a mysterious disease. The funerals and the suffering broke his heart – what could be causing it? Then he observed that they were all drinking water from the local pump so he crossed the road and removed the handle and gradually the plague subsided. The lesson is clear. If we offer friendship, food and much more to the homeless this is laudable but not enough. We need to ask what or who makes people and keeps people homeless and to my mind there are very definite reasons why the number of people on the streets and visiting the crypt has risen so dramatically. The sale of council houses and the lack of new-build rented accommodation is one reason yet the subject was hardly mentioned at the last election. To stop suffering and poverty we Christians need to get into politics and remove a few pump handles – not a very popular pastime but then hospitality is hard work.

Sometimes it is not always possible or appropriate to offer hospitality. In the very cold winter a few years ago a man started to build a cardboard house around one of the garden seats in our churchyard. Being a nice friendly Rector I did not move him on mainly because in reply to my question 'Should I get you into a hostel?' he pointed out that as I had never slept in a smelly dirty hostel perhaps I didn't realise my churchyard was more comfortable. The cardboard house got bigger and bigger as the weeks went by and in the end I had to move him on because I saw him showing some friends around it with a view to subletting. John Lee our priest counsellor got the Johnson Award for cleaning up the terrible mess he left behind. Fortunately most homeless people do want a home and do not want to live outside in this way.

'When you give a party do not invite your friends invite the poor.' These words of Jesus give me heart. If God is the Host, *I* certainly have no qualifications to come to His party, nor have any or us. We cheat, we forget and fail to love yet here we are at the party. George Herbert's poem 'Love bade me welcome' says it all. We shrink back from God the Lover, from his invitation, we are unworthy but we are still welcome.

> Love bade me welcome; yet my soul drew back,
> Guilty of dust and sin.
> But quick-ey'd Love, observing me grow slack
> From my first entrance in,
> Drew nearer to me, sweetly questoning
> If I lack'd anything.
>
> 'A guest', I answer'd, 'worthy to be here.'
> Love said, 'You shall be he.'
> 'I the unkind, ungrateful? Ah my dear,
> I cannot look on thee.'
> Love took my hand, and smiling did reply
> 'Who made the eyes but I?'
>
> 'Truth Lord, but I have marr'd them; let my shame
> Go where it doth deserve.'
> 'And know you not', says Love, 'who bore the blame?'
> 'My dear, then I will serve.'
> 'You must sit down', says Love, 'and taste my meat.'
> So I did sit and eat.

I was brought up in a Church which emphasised our wickedness and unworthiness all the time. At Mothball Mattins (the fur coat in front of me was overpowering) we were continually told how naughty we were. No one spoke to me as we left the church looking miserable because we had been at a Memorial Service for God. The truth is light years away from that Great Yarmouth horror story. Love bids me welcome. Jesus the Host says 'Come to the party. I accept you as you are,' so we take our seats at the table.

Outside the Gate

> *Jesus suffered without the gate. Therefore let us go to him without the gate bearing his reproach.*
>
> *Hebrews 13:10, 12-13*

My friends tell me I am good at getting other people to do things for me

– standing looking helpless with a hammer, nail or needle and thread in my hand until someone takes pity on me. However, there are good precedents for in my favourite Bible story Jesus, looking helpless, asked the woman at the well for a drink and got it. The story is magnificent and has many layers of meaning which are all unravelled in William Temple's commentary *Readings in St John's Gospel*. Jesus acknowledges his own needs – he is hot and tired and thirsty and he asks the woman to help him. What follows is breathtakingly direct . As Margaret Guenther points out in *Holy Listening* Jesus teaches the woman self knowledge and reveals her thirst for God. 'What I can give you will become in you a spring of water welling up to eternal life'. 'Give me that water' she says. 'I know the Messiah is coming'. 'I am He' says Jesus. She is not embarrassed by his knowledge of her chaotic sexual life, rather she learns from him what God wants her to do. Then she dashes to the village to share her excitement and we are told many people believed because of her.

The conversation at the well begins in practical down to earth terms and moves rapidly from physical to spiritual concerns, with water, symbol of refreshment and cleansing, as the unifying symbol.

The most telling point of the story for me is the startling fact that the Jewish Rabbi actually talks to a Samaritan woman of loose morals. Today it would be like asking a Jew and Arab to drink together or a Protestant and Catholic to embrace on the Falls Road. Jesus broke all the rules, Jews and Samaritans did not mix, men never talked to women in public and anyway, he certainly should not be talking to a person of such doubtful morals. She was an outsider and for me she represents everyone who has been marginalised because of their poverty, colour, gender or sexual orientation. There are so many outcasts in our society who live on the social, economic or ecclesial edges. Some by choice, most not.

Our text from the Letter to the Hebrews reminds us that Jesus was an outsider, crucified outside the city walls because his death on a cross would ritually pollute the townspeople of Jerusalem. All crucifixions had therefore to take place on the rubbish dump just outside the city gate, it seemed a fitting place to destroy human rubbish.

One of the most affirming letters I have ever received came from a devout woman who worshipped for a time at St Botolph's after being in a sort of spiritual wilderness. I have always thought that the congregation of St Botolph's, the gate church, consisted of several people either on their way in or out of the institutional church and she was coming in. She wrote, 'St Botolph's provided me with a way back when I was not sure which way I was heading spiritually. A church standing on the edge of the city and on the edge of the Church with special concern for vagrants, gays and Jews was just right for me. It meant much to be accepted.'

That is the vision I have of what the Christian Church should be – open, loving, welcoming to all and especially to those who feel hurt or rejected. Sadly Christians are often the very ones who push people outside, instead of welcoming them inside. At St Botolph's we do not have to look far to find women and men who are rubbished or ostracised. If you watch one of our colourful homeless men walking along the pavement you will see everyone gives him a wide berth. Incidentally, my mother had the same experience when Father died in 1978 and she asked me why everyone was avoiding her. 'Even people I know cross the road to get away,' she told me. Bereavement is embarassing to many, so better avoided.

How then can Christians 'go to Jesus outside the city gate bearing his reproach'? How can we stand with those who feel they are on the rubbish dump? Firstly by not joining in the general condemnatory clamour. I remember a priest in his eighties telling me he went to Michael Ramsey in the late 1920s when they both had just been ordained to ask for help about the horror of being homosexual. The future Archbishop, a shy stuttering academic was affirming, all loving. 'Society hates you, but God and Christians love you. Your orientation will bring many special gifts so use them to the full as you sublimate your sexuality.' The young priest went away rejoicing.

Stereotypes abound in our thinking – the homeless are workshy layabouts, the Irish fight, the Scots are mean, French are philanderers. But surely labels are for jam jars. If we put people into boxes it stops us learning the full story about that person and more seriously it reinforces their low self image. If you are constantly told you are worthless then soon you will feel worthless. In the crypt I hope we offer self respect because each person is a special creation of God, infinitely valuable in his sight. I remember John Vanier in a sermon stressing this and saying 'You are beautiful, you are beautiful.'

The women and men in our centre are 'outside the gate.' The single homeless we see are very ordinary people with stories of broken relationships, unemployment, depression, wanderlust and confused identity. As Pat Logan has pointed out in his splendid book, most of them are working class often with badly broken homes and backgrounds. They are people with a history of exploitation and low wages. Several have been in the Army, some are inadequate, alcoholic or mentally ill. Often they don't know their rights or what money they can claim, and often their difficulties are mainly due to external factors – government policies or economic forces.

So our workers and volunteers offer friendship, a big hug, some free food, a bath, a laundry and a chance to talk to a trained worker about accommodation, a job or a host of personal problems. A doctor or nurse is also on hand and sometimes a chiropodist who incidentally once gave me a lecture on feet – did I realise what walking all day does to you? Nowhere to sit, wash or sleep means you have to keep moving and that plays havoc with the feet especially if you are wearing ill fitting shoes.

Where does God come into all this? We are a Church, not a social work agency. Unlike some agencies we hand out no improving tracts and you do not have to attend a service to get a sandwich, thank God. However, speaking personally I found that as soon as I stepped into the canteen I was talking about God, the Church, morality and meaning in no time at all. Sometimes this could be embarrassing especially during a service in church when I would be forced into a dialogue sermon after someone shouted out, 'What about Henry VIII?' My worst experience was at the end of the very popular Harvest Festival Service when two gentlemen on either side of the aisle started abusing each other loudly, 'You're a f.... Catholic'; 'You're a f.... Protestant.' As the hymn ended liturgical breakdown seemed inevitable, so remembering my Army training I gained control by bellowing in a parade ground voice, 'If you want a Blessing – kneel down.' In a flash everyone including the combatants dropped to their knees.

Our task is of course to preach God in Jesus Christ and to share the good news of his teaching, death and resurrection and this will be done sensitively in our work of caring. But notice this. In the Gospels Jesus shows concern for the sick and the poor but he tells us it those who cause these evils who are in the greatest peril. He did not regard being oppressed as the ultimate evil, being the oppressor is far worse. So we must campaign against those who strip human beings of their dignity by exploitation, cruelty of oppression. Institutions made up of men and women are capable of great good or great evil, so they need reminding of their responsibilities.

Our Christian calling is to go outside the gate, stand alongside the marginalised and fight poverty, racism and hunger wherever we find it. There are however more serious states – unbelief and sin. Primarily our task is not to feed the hungry or fight oppression. These are the context in which we speak but they do not determine the content of our mission or its goal. The Gospel is about God. We certainly need bread, homes, dignity but above all we need God. From the Christian viewpoint being poor, being deprived, being oppressed are very serious misfortunes which the Gospel is meant to remedy but they are not final disasters. In the Biblical perspective sin matters more than poverty and guilt more than hunger.

Perhaps it is time that the many committees concerned with The Decade of Evangelism consider how the good news of the Gospel can be shared not only with those inside the respectable city but also with those who feel pushed out of the gate by Society or even by the Church itself.

Gay and Godly

A sermon preached at Great St Mary's, the University Church, Cambridge, 30 October 1988.

'The spirit of truth will guide you into all truth.'   John 16:13

It is condemned. It is expressly forbidden in Scripture. There are many condemnations in the Old Testament; not many in the New Testament. It is roundly condemned in the history of the Church. Four General Councils forbid such practices in clear rulings. Luther and Zwingli weighed against it. Until recently it was something distasteful to most men and women who are normal upright citizens. Scripture, Tradition and Reason – the three pillars of our authority as Anglicans are very clear on the subject.

What am I talking about? Well, I've bad news for Barclays, and the Bradford & Bingley Building Society and the Church Commissioners, because I'm talking about lending money at interest. Usury. Fortunately for the City of London, where I work, the Church has changed it mind. We're not quite sure when, sometime around Tudor times. Can the church change its mind if it is led by the Holy Spirit? 'The Spirit of Truth will guide you into all truth.' – my text for this evening.

Can the Church change its mind? That's one of the many questions the subject that I have been given tonight puts to you. On matters such as contraception, slavery, marrying divorced persons in church, and on usury the Church *has* changed its mind, because it believes the Spirit, the spirit of Jesus, the Spirit of God, has led us into all truth. New truth. So can one be gay and godly? I suppose we Christians have now become more gentle, so, unlike previous generations, many will say today that it's alright to be lesbian or gay by orientation, but you mustn't do anything about it – no genital acts. What an insulting phrase that is to most homosexual people. Judging their relationships solely by a below-the-belt morality. To me it says more about the judge than the judged. I believe it says that they're sick and they're unhealthy in their view of sexuality.

Scripture, Tradition and Reason, our three authorities, have indeed in the past condemned the homosexual to a life of celibacy, have forced a vocation on four percent of the population. This is a contradiction in terms because a vocation should surely be a voluntary response to a calling, not an enforced duty. Four percent is a conservative figure, But that would be around two and a half million men and women in this country today who are predominantly or exclusively homosexual. Four per cent. About the same percentage as the ethnic minority groups in our country today. We've not even begun to consider the bisexual, the person who in his orientation is seventy per cent/thirty percent, sixty per cent/forty percent.

So let us look at the three authorities that we have. Firstly Scripture. As with usury, so with homosexuality, there are many condemnations in the Old Testament. But all have to be read in the context of the times when they were written. We no longer stone people for collecting sticks on the Sabbath, nor, as far as I know, do most of us in church tonight keep the dietary laws. Are we then bound to the texts in the Old Testament which condemn the practices of homosexuality? Jesus said nothing specifically about homosexuality. Paul has three texts, and you can see the confusion regarding these if you compare the various Bible translations. Go into the local bookshop and open up the three texts and see how they're translated. Do they mean effeminate people in one translation? Child-seducers, people who pervert their true sexuality, for example heterosexuals who force themselves to experience homosexuality for kicks, for adventure? – is not Paul a child of his times, and did he in fact ever know any people in deep homosexual relationships? As I said at the beginning, when we look at this subject it throws into question all sorts of doctrines and one is, of course, the authority of Scripture. The Bible is indeed the most valuable thing that the world affords, but it is not an infallible book. There are plenty of erroneous beliefs in the Bible about astronomy, biology, geology, paleontology, but they have not invalidated or outdated the message of salvation in Scripture. For example the new knowledge which has enabled us to accept an evolutionary theory as we read Genesis, has not negated the message of Genesis, which is very clear – 'In the beginning God.' It has helped us to understand it more.

Scripture, Tradition. Professor John Boswell in his book *Christianity, Social Tolerance and Homosexuality* shows us that the Church has not always condemned homosexuals during its two thousand years of history. But nevertheless all major churches have condemned and continue to condemn any form of homosexual lifestyle other than celibacy. They feel very threatened if anyone suggests otherwise as I know to my cost. The Diocese of London, for instance, has succeeded in a shabby, disgraceful venture, using bigotry and antique ecclesiastical laws to force the Lesbian and Gay Christian Movement out of the office in my church of St Botolph. They've been there for twelve years. They were said to be porn peddlers and promoters of perverse practices – accusations too silly to reply to. In the Consistory Court to which I was summoned I was told that I had to throw myself on the mercy of the Court of the Chancellor. And quite honestly the atmosphere of the Consistory Court was a mixture of Toytown and Trollope.

Oh yes, I've occasionally regretted the Lesbian and Gay Christian Movement's robust tactics, and I honestly do wish they would be less aggressive and confrontational. But I do want to bear witness to the fact that they have helped literally hundreds of people put their faith and their sexuality together, and I don't see many other organisations doing that for homosexual people today. No, the Church and certainly the Diocese of London, is running scared and has acted accordingly. According to the rule of law. The Pope and Graham, Bishop of London – not a bad combination – believe that the sort of views LGCM put forward have a secular origin, and to hear them talk one would think that the organisation is advocating rape or theft or murder instead of helping people who love one another to care more deeply and responsibly for one another.

Scripture, Tradition and Reason. We ourselves using our own brains, our own experience under God to learn new truths. That's what I mean by reason. Until recently homosexual people have been invisible, but fortunately lesbian and gay people have escaped from the shadows over the last twenty years and have enabled us to share their experiences for the first time. This openness has of course been greatly hindered by the recent flood of homophobia unleashed by the onset of AIDS. People quite wrongly connect this disease solely with the homosexual world, and even the Church has been engulfed by homophobia. Just look at last November's General Synod. The final resolution that was put through talked of all homosexuals 'falling short of an ideal.' 'Who doesn't fall short? Thank God that today we now know more about homosexual people, and know that their relationships are just like anyone else's. Recently, in the United States twenty-three bishops signed a document saying that they had seen 'a redeeming quality in gay relationships which is no less a sign to the world of God's love than is the more visual sign of Christian marriage.' Sadly the bishops in this country do not share their feelings. Why don't they? Well, most of our bishops are public school boys, in their late fifties and sixties, who have experienced homosexuality in the dormitory as something shameful and shady, which is better forgotten, and today the only homosexual people most bishops meet are the naughty clergy who have been caught in a lavatory, or people who see their orientation as a problem. No wonder our bishops talk such nonsense on the subject. I doubt if any of them or very few of them, know any lesbian or gay committed couples, have experienced their friendship, have experienced their hospitality. And those bishops who are gay themselves, of course, are far too terrified to speak out at all.

Scripture, Tradition and Experience. Modern psychiatry is teaching us much on this subject. Are we prepared to listen? Is it God who is speaking? Or is it the Devil? We're learning today that the homosexual and heterosexual are not two separate and distinct entities, but two conditions, which like male and female merge together. There's a spectrum from male to female, heterosexual to homosexual, black to white, stupid to intelligent, Thatcher to Kinnock. Most of us know what we are, and the vast majority are of course heterosexual, but a significant number (and I think four percent is a very conservative figure) know that they are homosexual. There is no choice involved. One knows from the earliest days this is the way that one has been made. As one may be left handed or dark-haired. It's part of a natural creation, so it will be natural for a homosexual to make same-sex relationships, and it is the Church's responsibility, I believe, to help her or him to do it.

Now I realise I've been simplistic and brief in considering our three authorities, and how I believe God is teaching us new truths, but I hope that in our discussion and in our questions we can look more deeply and carefully into all three.

But let me now turn to pastoral care. What do we say to the individuals who come to us, for that after all is what Christianity is all about. Right relationships, with God and with each other. What do we say to lesbian and gay people who come to the Church for guidance? I recently read a first novel by Michael Carson, and it's called *Sucking Sherbert Lemons*. It's about a Catholic boy who is pathologically religious. (Some of us are, you know.) In his teens, he builds a house of faith, but then has to face the fact that he's homosexual. 'When I found out I was gay', he says, 'the whole house of cards fell down. I'd built up two floors and then when I realised what the Church says about gays, the attic roof fell in. And it brought the rest down with it. I'm a collapsed Catholic . . . Trying to make the best I can by searching though the rubble for something to call my own.' Well I think the Church should be ashamed of itself for allowing the collapse to take place. The fundamentalists still equate all homosexual acts with adultery and fornication. And one recently said to me, 'I suppose you'll be condoning sex with animals next.' Even the liberal bishops are still using words like 'handicapped.' A gay friend asked me if it means that he could park on double yellow lines. Now all those put-downs mean that unwittingly this sort of campaign is adding fuel to the fire of oppression and violence. Hardly a week goes by without a homosexual person being attacked on our streets. No doubt the attacker feels that he's got the Church's support. It is a cause of shame to me that few Christians are concerned with civil rights for gay people. There's no mention of it in the Gloucester Report of 1979 to the General Synod. Surely no matter what we think theologically about tonight's subject, we should be standing against the discrimination of gay people in employment and housing and education? Father Ken Leech, in a recent sermon uses the language of the Wild West to describe what he calls two types of Christians. The settlers and the pioneers. The settlers want to build a stockade around the faith, enforce it by lawcourts, and hold fast to what has been revealed by God. The pioneers want, under God to go out in their covered wagons on an adventure of faith. The wagon will fall off the road as new challenges are met and mistakes will be made, but what is wrong, for god's sake, with making mistakes? We're not politicians so we can admit to, and learn from our mistakes, as we seek to learn the new truths that God is showing us. 'The spirit of Truth will guide you into all truth.' Of course this subject is a new area of casuistry, so we need to tread carefully. Personally, I don't like looking at this one area of life in isolation.

I think what we need today in a theology of sexuality. We are so terribly confused in the Church on matters sexual. Up until now Christian teaching has been negative towards pleasure and positive towards procreation, and Catholic teaching still says that every act of intercourse should contain the possibility of procreation. Sex has been thought of as for creating children, and the pleasure that goes with it is no more than a suitable reward; whereas, of course, ninety-nine percent of sexual intercourse today is not for procreation. Sex in a relationship is usually for pleasure and for the binding together of the two people concerned. As Jack Dominian has said, 'sexual intercourse can be an act of reconciliation, thanksgiving, and affirmation.' So if we tackle the theology of sexuality we shall be called to reconsider homosexual persons. At present we say to them, I don't know much about you and the little I do know I don't like!

Now a few brief points to finish with. The first is that I think in discussing tonight's subject a massive programme of education is called for. We've got, as Canon Douglas Rhymes says, 'to educate the homosexual to the church,' somehow or other to say 'You are welcome'. Then we have got to educate the Church to the homosexual. For goodness sake stop shouting irrelevant slogans. Listen. Listen to the experience of homosexual people. And we have to educate the homosexual to the homosexual. It's no secret that the homosexual world is promiscuous but it's no good just tut-tutting. One's got to ask why. If someone's always been told that they're dirty and perverted and second class, they will behave like it. We have to help people realise that their love is indeed divine, and God has called them, created them to be lovers.

Secondly, I do want to affirm celibacy. It is a vocation and I have learned so much from the true celibate who has either lived in a Community or alone. It's given them enormous freedom, because they know where the boundaries are. But not everyone is called to that particular vocation.

And thirdly, spare a thought for the position of the gay clergy. Twice a year for the last twelve years I have organised a conference for clergy who are gay. Someone said we ought to hire the Albert Hall. At the meeting last Monday the level of anxiety and depression amongst the eighty or so who were there was very worrying indeed. Quiet honestly their life is becoming intolerable. A large part of themselves, perhaps the most important part, is hidden. Hidden from their employer, the bishop, and hidden from their congregation. It is not a life of integrity, and there are special problems for them because they have a public role in both church and society. Yet our inner cites are largely staffed by gay clergy and increasingly they are feeling unsupported, unaffirmed, harassed and even persecuted.

And fourthly and finally. Our Church today is rent asunder with all sorts of divisions and quarrels. I can quite understand why fewer are coming forward for full-time work, and why our congregations are falling. But I do not believe that the way forward is to un-church everyone who disagrees with you, whether it's about pacifism, the ordination of women, or the place of gay Christians in our Church or whatever. The Church of England has always been a broad church, but it seems to me that intolerance and bigotry are walking abroad today. Somehow we have got to learn to agree to disagree, on all sorts of subjects, or as Scott Peck puts it, 'to fight graciously' with those who disagree with us. Nothing will be gained by witch hunts or banging people over the head with the rule of law.

I'm sorry I've been so serious tonight, but it is a serious subject for us, but let me finish with a quote, a marvellous quote, which always has me in stitches. It's from a Victorian song that was sung in all the best drawing rooms. If only they knew what they were singing. It was a much-loved song of Richard Tauber but I won't sing it, I will say it to you to finish with.

Girls were made to love and kiss,
And who am I to interfere with this?
Am I ashamed to follow nature's way?
Can I be blamed if God has made me gay?

13 ST BOTOLPH'S TODAY AND TOMORROW

by The Revd Brian Lee, Rector of St Botolph's Aldgate

S t Botolph's Aldgate is unique in this country. It is the only church that has a Community Theologian. It is the only church that has an HIV and AIDS advisor. It is probably the largest staffed parish in the Church of England with its 35 full time staff servicing its work with homeless people in the City of London and the East End. The baton in the relay race of rectors was passed on to me on 14 July 1993.

Two months after my induction as the new rector a book by Michael de lay Noy entitled *The Church of England* was published that contained the extraordinary sentence, 'The Church of England at its very best can be seen in a parish such as St Botolph's Aldgate.' There can be no greater tribute to my predecessor Malcolm Johnson who during his eighteen years as Rector made this church famous throughout the world as one that cares for and values ALL people whatever their gender , sexual orientation, colour, class, physical or mental state. It has become and will continue to be a church that fights for justice and speaks for those who have no voice.

Our work in caring for homeless people continues to grow and develop. In September 1993 the Lodge Project , with its hostels in the East End of London and the St Botolph's Crypt Centre formally merged and the new organisation St Botolph's Project was formed. At the same time as this crucial change Richard Basch the Administrator and Daly Maxwell the Senior Social Worker both decided that the time was right for them to leave having worked in the crypt for 12 years. Both had been instrumental in making the crypt one of Londons premier homeless projects. Their contribution and dedication cannot be over emphasised. The project now has a new director John Downie who is in charge of the day to day running of our work with homeless people.

St Botolph's Aldgate is in the ward of Portsoken of the City of London. It is the most easterly of all the wards and follows the line of the ancient eastern wall of the City. In the centre of the parish and the ward was the Aldgate, the old entrance into the city from the east. Although the gate was demolished in 1760 a new gate has been created, this is in the form of the tight security cordon that protects the city from terrorist bombs and the eastern gap in the shield is on the very spot of the Aldgate where 24 hours a day police check all vehicles entering the vulnerable heart of the capital. This means that once again Aldgate is a bustling noisy and somewhat polluted entrance into the city.

Although a church has stood on the site for nearly a thousand years the present building was completed in 1744. This means that in the year of the publication of this history of Aldgate – 1994 – we will celebrate the fact that the present church has stood here for 250 years. The actual date of the opening of the building has proved impossible to find. There is no record in the Bishop of London's lists of consecrated churches of any consecration taking place at St Botolph's Aldgate! Who knows what the legal consequences of this anomaly may be?

On 27 January 1994 the City Churches Commission chaired by Lord Templeman produced their report to the Bishop of London. The Commission was set up with the following brief – 'within the mission strategy proposed by the Bishop of London, to consider the place of the parish and guild churches of the City of London in their pastoral and mission role; and to make recommendations regarding the practical and financial implications arising therefrom.' The fact that there are 36 churches in one square mile serving a resident population of only 5,000 people had to be faced seriously and honestly. The existence of so many churches for so few people has long been recognised as ludicrous and counter productive to any effective mission within the city. Even Charles Dickens who in the 1860s spent many a Sunday exploring 'the hidden and forgotten old churches in the City of London' later on in his book *The Uncommercial Traveller* commented that 'They remain like the tombs of the old citizens who lie beneath them and around them, monuments of another age.'

The Templeman Commission has produced an imaginative and brave recommendation in identifying twelve churches as active and deserving to be retained with clergy. The remaining twenty four are to be named 'reserve churches' that will still remain open to the public but will in due course change their use to other ecclesiastical or secular purposes perhaps as a concert hall, art gallery, library or livery hall. None will be demolished as all are listed buildings.

The Commission has recognised the essential work at St Botolph's and has recommended that the church be placed on the active list of city churches and to work in a group of three, the other two being All Hallows by the Tower and St Magnus the Martyr London Bridge. No-one knows whether the report will ever be implemented. What however is certain is that the future of our work is guaranteed and St Botolph's will continue to be that church on the edge, a bridge straddling the rich and powerful city and the poor and powerless East End. In the future St Botolph's will continue to be a church that takes as its vision the command of Jesus who washed his disciples feet and then said to them 'If I your Lord and Master, have washed your feet, you also ought to wash one another's feet.' John 13: 14

St Botolph's Aldgate

STAFF AT 21 MARCH 1994

The Revd Brian J. Lee	*Rector*
The Revd Elaine Jones	*Curate*
The Revd John Peirce	*NSM Priest Counsellor*
The Revd Ken Leech	*Community Theologian*
Br Colin Wilfred SSF	*HIV and AIDS Advisor*
The Revd Pat Wright	*NSM Parish Deacon*
The Revd Percy Coleman	*Lecturer*
Lee Willis	*Church Army Captain*
Philip Groom	*Reader*
Mary Everingham	*Verger*
John Bamford	*Organist*

ST BOTOLPH'S PROJECT

John Downie	*Director*

HIGH CARE - PARK LODGE

Pat Peart	*Co-ordinator*
Andrew Law	*Community Care Manager*
Doug Scott	*Senior Project Worker*
Christopher Socci	*Project Worker*
Charlotte Mason	*Project Worker*
James Francis	*Project Worker*
Nina Slaymaker	*PA to co-ordinator*
Brin Slaymaker	*Domestic Operator*

LOW CARE AND RESETTLEMENT

Barbara Townley	*Resettlement Team Leader*
Katrina Herbert	*Alcohol Resettlement Worker*
Eileen Crombie	*Mental Health Resettlement Worker*
Kenneth Sutherland	*Housing Support Worker*
Jonathan Bryant	*Resettlement Worker*

DAY CARE

Birgit Wagner	*Senior Social Worker*
Marie O'Kelly	*Social Worker*
Delrene Walker	*Social Worker*
Jo Robertson	*Social Worker*
Andrew Connell	*Advice Worker*
Robert Enlow	*Project Worker*
Robert Saint	*Project Worker*
Lee Willis (Church Army)	*Project Worker*
Christian Fussenegger	*Placement*

ADMINISTRATION

Tom Cohen	*Acting Administrator*
Sylvia Mellor	*Finance Manager*
Ruth McDermott	*Secretary*
Karen Stevens	*Secretary*
Andy Richardson	*Frontline Reception Worker*
Mary Everingham	*Cleaner*
Lily Cole	*Cleaner*

14 PRAY FOR US ST BOTOLPH

Pray for us as we travel.

We who feel ugly; unwanted.
When others turn away, or deride us.
Protect us.

We who have sinned; and will sin again.
We who are self-righteous.
Teach us.

We for whom no-one cares.
We who can care for no-one.
Be with us.

We who want to receive only the good things.
And to give nothing.
Show us.

We who are happy.We who mourn.
We whose bleeding, pleading hands are left empty.
Walk with us.

Guide us to walk together,
Even with those we want to hate.
And never looking back, with either gladness or regret.

That all people.
All peoples.
Shall travel in triumph.
Loving and praising God.

And, as we travel.
Pray for us, St Botolph.

Michael Williams

APPENDIX I

Parish Priests of St Botolph's and Holy Trinity Minories

The names of the Rectors of this parish in Saxon times have not yet been discovered, but when the church was given to the adjacent monastery some 40 years after the Norman Conquest the Priors were successively its Rector. Their names are easily discoverable and were as follows:

Norman	1108	Thomas Heron	1331
Ralph	1148	Nicholas de Aldgate	1340
Stephen	1170	William de Rysing	1377
Peter de Cornwall	1187	Robert Excetre	1391
Richard	1223	William Harrington	1408
John de Toting	1250	William Clark	
Gilbert	1260	John Sevenok	
Eustacius	1264	Thomas Pomery	
William Aynell	1280	Thomas Percy	
Stephen de Watton	1289	Richard Charnock	1507
Ralph de Canterbury	1302	Thomas Newton	
Richard de Wimbish	1314	John Bradwell	1513
Roger de Polay	1325	Nicholas Hancock	

Holy Trinity Priory, Aldgate, being dissolved in 1531 and its properties being distributed among the laity, the rectorship fell into lay hands and the parish priests were known as 'Vicares'. Their names, including those intruded by the Puritans, were as follows:

Robert Mason	1543	Edward Gadbold	1608
John Myles	1546	William Biddulph	1610
William Rofford	1548	Robert Prichett	1611
Richard Dabbes	1549	John Brigges	1611
Robert Heaz	1564	Samuel Bourman	1625
Christopher Threlkeld	1594	Thomas Edwards	1629
Paul Bush	1597	Thomas Swadin	1635
Henry Rigges	1604	(ejected 1642)	

Mr Vyner	1648	John Hutchinson	1722
Mr Rust	1650	Thomas Kynaston	1737
Laurence Wise	1654	Robert Wright	1765
John Mackerness	1655	Thomas Jackson	1783
Zachariah Crofton	1655	Henry Hutton	1796
Thomas Swadlin *(restored)*	1661	John Banks Hollingworth	1838
John Makerness *(restored)*	1662	Herbert Kynaston	1838
John Arden	1666	William Ludlow	1845
John Torbuck	1673	Richard Peace Baker	1846
Hugh Davis	1675	James Matthew Robertson	1860
Richard Hollingworth	1681	Robert Henry Hadden	1888
White Kennett	1700	James Francis Marr	1899
Thomas Bray	1708	J P R Rees-Jones	1939

The title of 'Rector' was restored to the parish priests of the City in 1952, the priests of those City Churches which were designated as Guild Churches remaining as Vicars. Since the restoration of the title the Rectors have been:

George Appleton	1957
Derek Harbord	1962
Malcolm Johnson	1974
Brian Lee	1993

Notes on some previous incumbents

THOMAS EDWARDS Born 1599, educated Queens College Cambridge. Puritan Divine suppressed and suspended for his views by Archbishop Laud. Minister of St Botolph's 1629-35. Died after many controversies in 1647.

WHITE KENNETT Educated St Edmunds Hall, Oxford. Rector of St Botolph's 1700-08. Archdeacon of Huntingdon 1701. Wrote a large number of pamphlets, sermons, books. Dean and later Bishop of Peterborough. 'He was courteous, bountiful and communicative. His application was intense, his judgement solid, his style easy and his elocution impressive.' He was three times married.

THOMAS BRAY Born 1656, educated All Souls, Oxford. Founder of the Society for Promoting Christian Knowledge (SPCK) and the Society for the Propagation of the Gospel (now USPG). In 1699 he went to Maryland USA and established free libraries as a missionary venture. On his return he established 80 parochial libraries in England. 1708-22 Vicar of St Botolph's. Died 1730.

JOHN BANKS HOLLINGWORTH Born 1780, educated Peterhouse Cambridge. DD 1819. Fellow 1807. Deacon 1804, priest 1804 (London). Vicar of Little St Mary's Cambridge 1807-14. Rector St Margaret Lothbury 1814-56. Incumbent St Botolph, Aldgate 1838, Archdeacon of Huntingdon 1828-56. Died 1856.

HERBERT KYNASTON Born 1810 the son of the Patron of St Botolph's. Educated Christ Church, Oxford. DD 1849. Rector of St Nicholas Cole Abbey 1850-66. Headmaster of St Paul's School 1838-76. Prebendary of St Paul's 1853. Incumbent of St Botolph's 1838-45. Died 1878.

WILLIAM LUDLOW Educated at Christ's and Peterhouse, Cambridge. Deacon 1829, priest 1830 (Lincoln). Curate of St Matthew Brixton 1841, and incumbent of St Botolph's 1845-46. Prebendary of Exeter Cathedral 1847-83. Overseas 1864-89. Died at Nice in 1889. Non resident rector of Kirton, Lincolnshire 1846-89.

RICHARD PEACE BAKER Educated at St John's Cambridge (?). deacon 1839, priest 1842 (Ely). Incumbent of St Botolph's 1846-60. Died 1860 in Syria from typhoid.

JAMES MATTHEW ROBERTON Born 1825, educated Magdalen, Cambridge. Deacon 1850, priest 1851 (Winchester). Incumbent of St Botolph's 1860 until his death in 1885.

ROBERT HENRY HADDEN Born 1854, educated Merton College, Oxford. Deacon 1877, Priest 1878 (London). Served curacies at St Mark North Audley Street and St George in the East. St Botolph Bishopsgate 1880-88, then vicar of St Botolph Aldgate 1888-98. He then returned to St Mark North Audley Street as vicar and chaplain to the Queen. Wrote a history of St Botolph's.

JAMES MARR Born 1868, educated at St John's College, Oxford. Deacon 1882, priest 1884 (Chester). Various curacies and teaching posts then curate of St Mark Hamilton Terrace, St Marylebone 1891-98. Incumbent of St Botolph's 1899-1939. Chaplain the Whitechapel Workhouse. Rural Dean, East City 1916-35.

GEORGE APPLETON Born 1902, educated Selwyn College,

Cambridge. Curate of St Dunstan Stepney. Worked in Burma 1927-46, incumbent of St Botolph's, 1957-61 then Archdeacon of London, Archbishop of Perth, then Archbishop of Jerusalem. Died 1993.

DEREK HARBORD (The Hon Mr Justice Harbord). Born 1902. Educated Grays Inn and St Michael's Llandaff. Various ecclesiastical appointments until 1935 when he became a Roman Catholic and practised at the English Bar. 1953-59 Judge of the High Court of Tanganyka. Lecturer at Ghana School of Law 1959-61. Rejoined Church of England, 1960. Rector of St Botolph's 1962-74. Recreations listed in *Who's Who*: '15 grandchildren, reading modern theology and other who-dunnits.' Died 1987.

MALCOLM JOHNSON Born 1936, educated University College, Durham. Chaplain to Queen Mary College London 1967-74. Rector of St Botolph's 1974-92. Area Dean of the City 1985-90. Master of The Royal Foundation of St Katharine 1993 onwards.

INCUMBENTS OF HOLY TRINITY MINORIES

1563	Will Park	1661	Elkanah Downes
1578	Robert Hearse	1666	Thomas Lunn
1578	Thomas Cobhead	1678	John Weston
1590	David Inglishe	1694	John King
1595	John Glass	1720	John Morrice
1597	James Meadowes	1721	Thomas Kinnersley
1598	Thomas Smith	1729	Robert Palmer
1602	Gabriel Boult	1747	William Petvin
1608	Richard Swinnerton	1756	Thomas Newman
1617	George Calvert	1770	Henry Fly
1619	Robert Johnson	1834	William Blunt
1619	Robert Challacomb	1850	Thomas Hill
1619	Jonas Stuckton	1865	William Green
1621	Christine Sherwood	1877	Edward Tomlinson
1633	John de Cerfe	1889	Samuel Kinns
1634	Timothy Bracegirdle	1899	James Marr

(First Vicar of the United Benefice of St Botolph with Holy Trinity)

APPENDIX II

The Aldermen of Portsoken Ward

The 27 Priors of Holy Trinity, Aldgate were the jure officio Aldermen of Portsoken Ward from 1108. After the suppression of that monastery they were succeeded in the Aldermanry as follows.

1538	Henry Averall	1659	William Love
1538	John Wylford	1662	Sir Thomas Bloodworth
1542	George Barne	1664	Henry Hampson
1546	Henry Goodyere	1664	Sir Samuel Starling
1549	Thomas Offley	1674	Sir James Smyth
1550	Lawrence Wythers	1687	Sir Richard Hawkins
1557	Thomas Rowe	1687	Sir John Parsons
1560	Edward Banks	1688	Sir James Smyth
1566	Ambrose Nicholas	1689	Thomas Papillon
1569	Philip Gunter	1690	Sir John Wildman
1569	Henry Myllies	1693	Sir William Hedges
1574	William Kympton	1701	Sir Jeffrey Jefferies
1580	Ralph Woodcock	1709	William Andrew
1584	Stephen Slanye	1710	Edmund Noble
1586	Henry Prannell	1710	Richard Dyer
1588	Giles Garton	1711	Sir John Cass
1589	Richard Gourney	1718	John Green
1594	Edward Fisher	1721	Humphrey Parsons
1602	Sir William Romenay	1741	Sir William Calvert
1605	George Holman	1761	Hon Thomas Harley
1605	John Leman	1785	Sir Benjamin Hammett
1616	Cuthbert Hacket	1798	Sir James Shaw
1624	Robert Parkhurst	1832	William Hughes
1634	John Highlord	1833	Thomas Johnson
1639	Thomas Adams	1844	David Salomons
1641	Thomas Keighley	1844	Sir Francis Moon
1642	John Langham	1871	Sir Thomas White
1648	Richard Bateman	1883	Sir Henry Isaacs
1649	George Hadley	1891	Sir Marcus Samuel
1649	Richard Chiverton	1921	Isidore Jacobs
1652	Andrew Cade	1933	Sir Samuel Joseph
1652	Edward Smith	1946	Sir Keith Joseph
1652	Thomas Merry	1949	Sir Bernard Waley-Cohen
1653	William Beake	1984	Sir Peter Keith Levene
1653	William Thomson		

BIBLIOGRAPHY

George Appleton, *Unfinished*, Collins, 1990.

AGB Atkinson, *St Botolph Aldgate*, Grant Richards, 1898.

Gordon Barnes, *Stepney Churches*, Faith Press, 1967.

JA Dodd, *Troubles in a City Parish Under the Protectorate*, Spottiswoode, 1895.

GV Bennett, *White Kennett*, SPCK, 1957.

Chaim Bermant, *Point of Arrival*, Methuen, 1975.

Thomas Rogers Forbes, *Chronicle from Aldgate*,Yale, 1971.

William J Fishman, *The Streets of East London*, Duckworth, 1979.

William J Fishman, *1888*, Duckworth, 1988.

E. Freshfield, *The Communion Plate of the Churches in the City of London*, Rixon and Arnold, 1984.

HJ Griffin, *History of Ward of Portsoken*, Pamphlet, Waterlow & Layton, 1884.

Harvey Hackmans, *Wates's Book of London Churchyards*, Collins, 1981.

Adam Joseph, *Petticoat Lane*, 1975.

Samuel Kenns, *Holy Trinity Minories*, 1890.

Pat Logan, *A Life to be lived. Homelessness and pastoral care.* DLT, 1989.

GE Morrison, *St Botolph Aldgate*, pamphlet, Graham Cumming, 1958.

Denys Pegg, *Rowbotham House*, pamphlet, Pearl Assurance, 1985.

Charles Padgham, *The Organ of St Botolph's Aldgate*, pamphlet available at St Botolph's Bookstall, 1975.

N Pevsner, *The Buildings of England Vol. 1*, Penguin Books, 1966.

George Ryan, *Botolph of Boston*, Christopher, USA, 1971.

Donald Rumbelow, *The Houndsditch Murders*, St Martin's Press, Macmillan, 1973.

Donald Rumbelow, *The Complete Jack the Ripper*, WH Allen, 1976.

George Tull, *North of the Tower*, 1974.

HP Thompson, *Thomas Bray*, SPCK 1954.

Edward Tomlinson, *A History of the Minories*, Murray, 1922.

Isobel Watson, *Gentlemen in the building line*, Padfield Publications, 1989.

Ed. Weinreb and Hibbert, *The London Encyclopedia*, Book Club Associates, 1983.

 Other publications from Stepney Books

MY POPLAR EASTENDERS
by Carrie Lumsden, £4.95, illustrated
Insight into life as a child in Poplar during the First World War
0 9505241 7 4

EDITH AND STEPNEY
by Bertha Sokoloff, £4.95, illustrated
The life of Edith Ramsay. Education, politics and social change in
Stepney 1920-79.
0 9505241 6 6

MEMORIES OF OLD POPLAR
by John Blake, £1.20, illustrated
Poplar family and street life between the Wars.
0 9505241 1 5

CHILDREN OF THE GREEN
by Doris M Bailey, £3.95, illustrated with line drawings
Cheerful autobiographical portrait of Bethnal Green family and street
life between the Wars.
O 9505241 4 X

IN LETTERS OF GOLD
by Rosemary Taylor, £4.95, illustrated.
The story of Sylvia Pankhurst and the East London Federation of the
Suffragettes in Bow.
0 9505241 8 2

BRICK LANE 1978
by Ken Leech, £3.95, illustrated.
The anti-fascist struggle against the National Front (updated in the
light of events 1993-94).
0 950524 9 0

All the above books can be ordered from:
Stepney Books Publications, 19 Tomlins Grove, London E3 4NX.

Postage extra on small orders. Usual trade terms.

*Stepney Books Publications is a community publishing group producing East
End history and autobiography.*